GREG HELMER

Lead with Endurance

26.2 Milestones for Improving Life and Leadership

First edition

ISBN: 978-1-7344579-1-9

Illustration by Cynthia Palmer
Editing by Elizabeth Prentice
Proofreading by Carrie Helmer
Cover art by Danielle Benedict

This book was professionally typeset on Reedsy.
Find out more at reedsy.com

Contents

I   THE HURDLES

II   THE MILESTONES

Praise for Lead with Endurance

"Challenges in our personal and professional lives are inevitable. *Lead with Endurance* provides the necessary tools to endure the discomforts of life and leadership. Greg's book will leave you with a mindset and drive to succeed, learning and growing from each milestone along the way."

- Jon Gordon, author of *The Power of Positive Leadership* and *The Energy Bus*

"*Lead with Endurance* is not just a book, it's a guide that includes 26.2 proven lessons that will transform your mindset and provide lessons on how to live and lead without being afraid of facing challenges. From book studies of small cohort groups to entire organizations, Greg's stories and milestones provide a framework for thinking, leading, and enduring."

- Brian Diemer, 3-Time Olympian, Track and Field, USA Team , 1992

"Greg successfully manages his Tourette's Syndrome, has conquered treatment for a brain tumor and rose above the loss of a highly public position. *LwE* is a book that will quickly catch your attention while providing a long-lasting impression of how to live and lead."

- Dr. Chad Uptigrove, D.O., Core Faculty for Family Medicine Residency Program and Family Physician

"I have known Greg Helmer for 30 years. During those three decades, I have witnessed his performance as a competitor, teacher, coach, and administrator. At each step in his professional "race", he has embodied what a leader should be - someone who enhances the lives of those around him. Greg lives and breathes inspiration and those he works with [leads] are uplifted by his energy, enthusiasm, and vision. LwE is not only a great story of how Greg developed into the leader he is today but also an invaluable resource for those striving to learn, lead and live with endurance. The milestones Greg describes in this book when applied will improve learning, growth, and endurance for leaders and entire organizations."

– Dr. Brad Kahrs, Associate Professor – Mathematics Education, University of Wisconsin – Stevens Point

Dedication

Without a doubt, I am blessed with an amazing family.

To my wife, Carrie, you're the Thelma Ray of the next generation. Thanks for enduring life and leadership with me as God continues to guide our journey. You. Me. Together...Forever! I love you.

To Hayden, Jackson, and Landon... know that your faith in God will allow you to endure every challenge you face. The challenges are often unpredictable, but God's presence is always present. Each of you brings pure joy to all of our lives.

To my mom and dad, Art and Janet, thanks for your unconditional love, support, guidance, and role modeling. Your gift of showing us how to endure the challenges of life with faith and perseverance has become the theme of my *LwE* project. Thanks for believing in me through all of my hurdles and milestones.

To my other mom and dad...Big Jer and Cindy, thanks for accepting me as a son of your own and showing all of us what "giving" truly means. Your hearts are full of giving and our family bond is tight because of your relentless passion for family-first mentality. I love our Saturday evening tradition...Family!

Foreword by David Hulings

I am hopeful that by reading *Lead with Endurance: 26.2 Milestones for Improving Life and Leadership* you will accomplish the following:

- Understand that growth can occur in amazing ways when you don't see yourself as a victim of challenges, but rather as someone who overcomes challenges!
- Become inspired to endure the obstacles of life and leadership.
- Develop specific action steps to move your leadership forward with growth by learning 26.2 milestones to assist you in life and leadership.
- Inspire others and make an impact on those you lead by developing influence with family, friends, and colleagues.
- Ultimately, through challenges, build stamina, a "Lead with Endurance" mindset in whatever "race" you encounter.

Endurance? Life is tough. Leadership can be rough. It takes endurance to live and lead. For most of Greg's life, he has focused on building endurance by living, leading, and learning through the disciplined habits of an endurance runner. As Greg continues to transition through his career in educational leadership, he has reaffirmed now more than ever that endurance is the key to being a successful leader. Endurance is not simply the ability to persevere through a difficult situation, but to find joy and glory in knowing that you did not surrender! Greg continues to find joy knowing that God continues to use his talents and skills to impact others.

Life and leadership are like running a race. The process and journey of training for the race are often overlooked by runners, which is the most significant part of any training plan. As with runners, leaders sometimes find themselves too quick to focus on results without the will, discipline, stamina, or drive to endure the most critical piece...the process of training for a race. While there are sure to be struggles during the race, it's the suffering and journey of training for weeks, months, and sometimes years for a specific race that provides pure joy. It's the daily grind of fighting the elements of adverse weather conditions, running in the predawn hours when it's raining or snowing, doing hill repeats up a sand dune until the legs and lungs burn with pain, and the healing from injuries that build endurance. Life and Leadership are no different, if we can focus on the process, which truly is the race, no finish line banner or finish time will exceed the joy of knowing that you endured. Leadership is a process. Like running a race, each race has milestones. Milestones in leadership are accomplished by moving forward one step after another; leading, influencing, and impacting others toward a common finish line.

Leadership is messy, sometimes exhausting, and if privileged enough, painfully tough because of the love, passion, and care you have for those you lead and the organization in which you lead. Like races, there are a variety of distances, different terrains to conquer, and unexpected surprises that may drop you to your knees. Sometimes, we must recognize when it's time to find a different racecourse or even learn a new process of training. Because of passion, relationships, and genuine love for the work, each departure is memorable for a leader. As a runner, there is always another race to enter and with leaders, sometimes our race ends when the finish line has yet to be crossed.

It's inevitable that if you have not endured pain in your personal life or professional life, the time will come. Life and leadership will cause pain and suffering, but through the suffering, great learning, growth, and improvements lie ahead, once you find a way to endure.

For too long, Greg had been able to avoid major pain and suffering. Of course, there were moments of obstacles, difficult times, and troubles, but I am not talking about the types of "minor" setbacks or struggles. I am talking about significant, drop you to your knees, deep mourning type of life-changing experiences that become profound enough to shift your priorities and purpose in life as a leader. Greg has endured through his faith in God and his leadership lessons in *LwE* are incredibly practical for any leader.

While it was not clear for Greg during his time of mourning the news of a brain tumor and losing a highly public position, the clarity and profound impact on him personally and professionally has been something I am forever grateful for. I am grateful that through God's grace, Greg endured difficult times, and continues to lead and live in ways that impact others for a greater purpose.

LwE was written with the hope of inspiring others to endure the obstacles we will all uniquely and undoubtedly face. Join Greg in his journey by reading, processing, and discussing each milestone at your own pace. Greg has organized each milestone with reflection questions, presented in a way that will impact your leadership and those you lead with an inspiring voice of a man who is devoted to his faith, family, and professional career as a leader in education.

David Hulings

CEO, Hulings & Associates - Motivational Transition Coaching for Leaders Author of Just Middle Manager - Next Great Leader

Acknowledgements

Beth Prentice: My first memory of Beth was when I was coaching track and field at a neighboring high school. Beth was a school record holder in the 1600 meter run, and I was assisting my former collegiate coaches with recruiting her to attend Calvin College. Not only did Beth attend Calvin College, but I was also fortunate enough to work with her when I became the Principal at Mona Shores Middle School. It did not take me long to realize that Beth had developed into a national class teacher, and I was incredibly grateful when I was able to convince Beth she would be an awesome teacher leader by becoming a department chair for Language Arts. Beth flourished as a leader and her insight on the culture and climate in our building kept me in the loop on healthy decision making for our students and staff.

Nearly three months after I resigned from being the Superintendent of Mona Shores Public Schools, Beth and I met at a coffee shop to discuss the manuscript for *LwE*. I am forever grateful for the countless hours of editing, suggestions, and ideas Beth provided me via Google Docs throughout the winter of 2018. Most of Beth's assistance was after a full day of teaching, and after her two children were tucked into bed for the night. Beth was an editor with endurance!

Thank you, Beth, for the just in time messages of encouragement along the journey. You're an amazing person and educator!

Bill Trujillo: Bill is one of the finest educational leaders I know. Bill is a former head wrestling coach at Purdue University and retired from public education after years of impacting school culture as a principal and superintendent. Bill continues to inspire me with his thought-provoking conversations, and his ability to connect with people is quickly recognized upon meeting him.

Thank you, B.T., for the countless breakfast chats in Grand Haven during my desperate searches to find a job after my resignation, and during my book-writing adventure. I wish every teacher could be as fortunate to have a principal like you during their career!

My wife, **Carrie**: Thank you for believing in me. Without your nudging, support, and countless hours of cleaning up my mistakes, LwE would not be possible. I hope LwE impacts not only a greater audience than you and I can imagine but future generations within our family. You. Me. Together. Forever...

"No need to wish for an easy road in life; live and lead building strength to endure a difficult one! Do what is right, which might be challenging, not what is easy! If what is right is also easy, count it as a blessing."

Greg Helmer

Introduction

In the fall of 1987, I was introduced to the sport of cross country running during my sophomore year of high school. While the thought of running five kilometers back then seemed insurmountable, what I didn't realize at the time, was how distance running would eventually become one of my greatest analogies for life and leadership lessons. Running is not easy. It takes endurance (mental and physical) to be a successful runner. It takes endurance to live life. Enduring the demands of any leadership position and living through the milestones of life, work, and family requires stamina.

As a first-year runner, what I didn't realize is how building endurance takes time, effort, and miles and miles of pounding the pavement. Building endurance does not come easy, but with consistent dogged training, the body begins to increase stamina and more importantly, the will of the mind strengthens. By incrementally increasing both workload and mileage, endurance is built. Endurance, however, is a variable phenomenon. The unknown factor of how much you can increase your endurance is paralleled by how much you are willing to train. The mind is challenged to overcome the pain of training and here potential becomes realized!

For athletes, the body and mind develop over time, building endurance to sustain the suffering of training, injuries, setbacks, and hurdles. For each of us, our endurance is built by unique experiences and backgrounds.

Personally, my endurance training for running became the pool of strength I have drawn from to endure the suffering of setbacks. How did I create this pool of strength? As a young kid, I journeyed for hours and hours and miles and miles on my dirt bike and later, a four-wheeler, along the powerlines and spider web of trails south of the Muskegon River in Michigan. I relished this time of exploring, being free, and simply allowing my mind to roam. Taking rides on my dirt bike and four-wheeler were milestones of habitual thinking and meditating. I recall reciting my multiplication problems while riding up "Shot-gun" hill, which was a towering sand dune that locals would use as a backstop when target practicing and sighting in their firearms. Mighty "Shot-gun" hill was long enough and harrowingly steep enough to present an intimidating challenge each time I was bold enough to throttle up. Cruising along those Muskegon River trails provided me with a respite for reflection on school and relationships. These woodland rides were a gift - a simple yet powerful distraction from the social pressures and temptations a boy encounters while growing up. I also had a childhood friend, Chad Latsch, who spent hours on those hallowed trails with me. The tanks of gas we emptied kept our parents busy at the pump. During the middle school years, many of my friends attended sleepovers and parties, often drinking alcohol and seeking thrills by finding trouble. To avoid the pressure, I lost myself on the trails, often on Friday and Saturday nights and well into the dark, shining for deer with my spotlight as I thrashed through the brush. I used the freedom of riding that motorized four-wheeler to feed the desire that teenagers seek...freedom, independence, and control. Avoiding certain peer groups as a teen, while lonely at times, provided the opportunity for my mind to think, dream, plan, and reflect. I certainly did not recognize it at the time, but my mind was building endurance.

But the real physical and mental endurance did not begin until my legs became the motor. During the summer of 1988, I quickly transitioned from a four-wheeler to a pair of running shoes, and I began hitting the same trails but with a different purpose. I spent hours and hours, miles and miles, running the power lines between Hall Road and US 31, hitting every trail I could find, hellbent on building my endurance. Despite playing junior varsity basketball during my sophomore year, I was struggling with exercise-induced asthma. Long runs sent me sputtering for air, chest tight, breaths were jagged. Why would a wheezing, inhaler-dependent kid insist on the challenge of distance running? At times my asthma was so severe, I couldn't make laps in gym class unless I had that trusty albuterol inhaler. Without Coach Nash and Coach Graham teaching me how to build my endurance, the importance of nutrition, resilience, and a commitment to training, I would have easily quit my career as a distance runner. Reflecting on this struggle, I am reminded of Randy Pausch's powerful statement, "The brick walls are not there to keep us out. The brick walls are there to show us how badly we want something." Quitting is so easy to do when faced with an adverse challenge. Asthma strangled my progress. A focused training run would succumb to a stagger and end in a panic attack, gasping for air to my desperate lungs. The hurdles of adversity exist to test our determination and grit. Over the ensuing weeks, months, and miles, I remember how my endurance began to improve. Running five kilometers no longer felt uncomfortable. I knew I was building endurance when it would often take me three to four miles before I would actually begin feeling "good' when I was out on a training run. Steady breathing merged with my swift pace, replacing my once exploding lungs and labored shamble. I was flying past mile markers where my pace and spirit once used to crumble. Consistently, I began to increase my weekly mileage from 20 miles to 35 miles. My long run reached eight miles, and I accomplished my first major goal of running 350 miles between Memorial Day and Labor Day.

On Labor Day of 1988, I was running along a trail between "Shotgun Hill" and my school, Gustafson Elementary, when I faced my first injury as a distance runner. I was running on a makeshift bridge across a creek, constructed from pallets and scrap wood. As my foot came down on a rotted board, my ankle crashed through the hole, catching a nail and staples, ripping my shoe off, tearing through my sock, and piercing my toes and ankle.

I dropped to the ground to assess the damage. Peeling off my sock, I plunged my mangled foot in the creek. Blood gushed from my toes; I used my other sock to clean the torn mess. As I stood, searing pain shot in waves from my swelling ankle. Crumpling back to the ground, I thought about the 350 miles I had just celebrated, only to be eclipsed by an injury. The classic: "Why me?" and "Why now?" thoughts raged. Would I be able to race in the first meet of the season? Without any option but to get up, I stood and leaned into a hobble. Only two miles from home, if I could make it out to MacArthur Road, I could hitch a rescue ride home. I tottered along for a half-mile, eventually making my way to my elementary school. Collapsing onto a bench, I gingerly tested that ankle. First with a hesitant stretch and then into circular motions, but the swelling and pain were overwhelming. Blood filled my sockless-shoe, and I just broke down. The pain was one thing, but the fear that I was going to miss not just the first race of the cross country season but perhaps the entire season was too much to hold. Tears for my wasted work poured.

I loosened my shoestrings around the mad swelling and urged myself forward. Foolishly, I worked into a run, shuffling down MacArthur towards Brooks Road for nearly a mile, finally slowing to a walk about a half-mile from home. Angry horse flies buzzed around my sweaty head, and I crashed to the cement at the end of someone's driveway, my ankle aflame. I thought for a moment, maybe I could crawl home. Too proud, stubborn, or embarrassed to crawl, I hopped in agony on one leg until I collapsed at our doorstep. Later, icing my sprained ankle and soaking my torn toes, I thought of how stupid I was for "running" nearly two miles in such a condition, but little did I know, I was being conditioned to endure pain and suffering, a trait that is necessary for living life and leading in any role. While I didn't get to compete in the first two meets of the year due to my injury and cuts on my toes and foot, turning my ankle on a makeshift bridge across a creek was truly the turning point of my endurance.

As a distance runner, I have learned to keep going; pushing and driving forward even when it's painful and difficult. Sometimes the weather is miserable, but I lace up my shoes and push out the door. Sometimes I feel sick or have some soreness, but I find a way to log the miles and keep grinding. Sometimes my mind tells me not to run by making up excuses. One thing for sure, I have never regretted a run. I have yet to think of a run as a waste of time or felt displeased because I completed a workout – there is sweetness in the slog. Ironically, the miles I have been most reluctant to run always turn out to be the most glorious. Some may call the feeling a "runner's high," I call it progress; knowing I persevered with another milestone completed. Finishing a run is always gratifying for me, bringing vigor to my body, soul, and spirit!

Training has made me feel alive since 1987, the year I laced up my first pair of running shoes. Training builds endurance, which in turn, has compelled me to keep going, one step after another, one milestone after another. I have endured multiple challenges while running, challenges that have instilled in me a character deep down in which I refuse to surrender. There are not many guarantees in life and leadership; however, one sure thing is that we will all face struggles in which our minds will tell us to give up. While it's inevitable that pain and suffering will occur in life and in our careers, the milestones you will encounter by reading *Lead with Endurance* will groom your mindset to be one that persists. Surrendering is not an option because when you look in the mirror, your reflection will tell you whether or not you quit. For in our minds, we know whether or not we have surrendered or endured the pain and suffering to the best of our ability.

Life is hard. Leadership is hard. Pain is inevitable as we live and lead. Similarly, running is hard, but the pain is avoidable by not running. Runners welcome pain and learn to endure the discomforts that are inevitable. The difference between life and living and the demands of running is that runners have an awareness of the time, duration, level, and location of the pain. Life and leadership are filled with surprises that cause pain, but one thing we know for sure...Leadership takes time to develop just as endurance takes time to build for an athlete. Not only do we condition the body, but we also condition the mind, and it's our mind that allows us to endure pain, suffering, and challenges. *Lead with Endurance (LwE)* is a mindset, a will, a drive to succeed, a mission to finish the race, learning and growing from each milestone along the way. When we "Lead with Endurance," the impact is life-changing, and the finish line is celebratory! Consider running as a metaphor to life, and no worries if you have not run a step since the days your physical education teacher made you run the dreaded mile back in high school. Whether you have run a 5K, a marathon, or have not run a race in your life, *Lead with Endurance* is not about running, it's about living and leading. Running is simply the connector that I have used for how I live and lead. Your "running" could be a host of worthy pursuits from cycling to bird-watching—the point is that your "running" will be a valuable metaphor for your life and leadership.

The Marathon

Tough training runs build endurance in a way that we become capable of facing any challenge that comes our way. Running is not glamorous. Running is hard work and it hurts. The willingness to welcome discomfort and to do hard things while running makes it easier to endure obstacles in our non-running lives. In a Tweet by Desi Linden, one of America's best distance runners, she posted, "We all run at different paces and for different reasons but the activity remains the same — right foot, left foot, repeat. I try and use my 'platform' to remind people the running experience is pretty universal and all-inclusive." For some runners, the marathon becomes a lure as the ultimate physical and mental challenge. Whether a runner or not, the marathon is understood as an ultimate test of endurance. Training not only builds endurance but develops character and determination to persevere pain and suffering. From tendinitis and chafing to running in rain and snow, enduring discomfort cannot be faked when training for or running a marathon. The distance of a marathon is 26.2 miles and each milestone presents a unique test of character that is not found in shorter distances, or in any other physical activity in which I have attempted. Enduring the many months of training for a marathon presents struggles, and on race day, despite the preparation, the mind and body will experience pain and suffering unlikely ever felt before. Marathons are long enough that you might not finish the race due to challenges that can occur when running for several hours. Hundreds, sometimes thousands, of runners do not finish the race they start...they cannot endure the pain or suffering despite the months of training. Because of the discomfort, they surrender. Even though some may finish a marathon, they may become heartbroken by not reaching a specific goal of time or place.

Running 26.2 miles is daunting. Leadership is daunting. If we do not allow our limits to be tested - the opportunity to test what we are made of, the gut-wrenching, soul-centering moments of pushing past excruciating pain - we will always shrink from realizing our true potential. Leadership is not a sprint where immediate rewards are obtained after a brief effort. Leadership is a marathon, the unrelenting, steadfast, adamant refusal to soften when it becomes difficult. There are no quick rewards; the glory comes only after many arduous gritty miles.

Fun Fact - Marathon is a city in Greece. Legends have been shared that after the Athenians defeated Persian invaders at the Battle of Marathon in 490 B.C., a messenger ran nearly 26 miles to report out on the victory. The runner, whose name was Pheidippides, actually ran the distance from Marathon to Athens, which is about 40 kilometers...just under 26 miles. The distance caused a great amount of pain and suffering and just after mustering the words, "We won", he fell down and died. The Persians later surrendered, possibly out of fear of the superpowers portrayed by the Athenians. Although there isn't any proof of this legend, the story provided enough inspiration in which the competition of the marathon occurred for the first time in the 1896 Olympic Games.

Since 1987, I have completed countless races: cross country, track, and road races. However, NONE of the races I ever completed inflicted as much pain as the marathon. I started training specifically for the marathon on January 1st, 2001 with the goal of running the 2001 Chicago Marathon. Until this point, I was truly a middle-distance runner, preferring track meets and racing my favorite distances: the mile and 800 meters. Finding road races just about every weekend, I rarely raced more than 5 kilometers. I enjoyed the challenge to see how much pain I could endure during these "short" distances. But on October 7, 2001, I endured a new level of pain I had never experienced.

The Chicago Marathon is known for its flat, fast course. In 2001, I faced my first marathon with an eager and ambitious heart, but the emotion was palpable among the record-breaking 37,500 people who pinned their racing numbers on for this pinnacle event. Our country had just endured the terrorist attacks of 9/11 and the raw distress could be seen, heard, and felt all around the streets of Chicago. Gnawing fears stemmed from both the sheer demand of the 26.2 miles but also the alarming dismay that hundreds of thousands were gathered together in one of America's greatest cities for this iconic event. Were we running targets? What made this event even more memorable, yet caused heightened fear for my wife and I was that our first-born son was with us on the trip. Hayden was less than two months old, and he too was prepared to endure the cool temps, raging crowds, and adventure right along with his dad. For many reasons, the playing of the national anthem gave me chills, and for a moment, the buzz of nearly a million spectators and runners became silent. The 2001 Chicago Marathon was another historic race – a record number of runners, more than 950,000 spectators, a pacer surprising all by winning, and a new women's World Record was set.

Finishing 381 overall and averaging 6:34 per mile for 26.2 miles was all I could endure on that day, every fiber of my being was spent. I ran incredibly well for 20 miles, right on my target goal of running sub 6:30 pace, but I can tell you that by mile number 23, I wanted to quit. The pain was unlike any I had ever felt before. My lower body felt as if I was lifting elephant legs each stride, and my quads, calves, and hamstrings screamed in agony each time I pushed with every ounce of energy I had. The pain you feel during a marathon is an entirely different kind of threshold. The sense of inflammation and microscopic muscle tears in every connecting tissue seems to scream, "QUIT!" You are completely drained of all physical, emotional, and mental strength. Every muscle fiber in your legs feels totally used up, and they hurt clear to the bone. My stomach was cramping, causing me to dry heave twice, but I kept telling myself you run with your legs, not your stomach. It was a hellish battle of might and drive, telling myself to move the legs faster when they spoke back with repulsiveness. My arms, shoulders, and neck joined the internal battle, sending messages of surrendering to the torment and torture I felt. For nearly three miles, my mind was telling me to walk off the course, sit on the curb, or just lay down. Despite the pain, I continued to move forward, one milestone after the next, sometimes breaking the milestones down into the next turn, the big blue sign ahead, or even better, the next competitor. Passing competitors who were falling back because the pain was too much for them to endure, kept me chugging forward...anything to keep my mind from giving up. Finally, I could see the finish line, while a bit wobbly, suffering miserably, I recall the feeling of euphoria when hearing over the public address system blaring the streets of downtown Chicago, "Congratulations, you just finished the Chicago Marathon!" I crossed the line and was greeted by medical attention and escorted to a table, too unsteady to walk on my own. Entirely depleted...my legs could not move...I had nothing left. But in that state of stumbling delirium, I knew that I could look in the mirror knowing I could not have run a second faster...I conquered the marathon!

At times, I believe Western culture has things backward. Far too many people are not willing to "run the marathon before the battle". Too many people seek the comforts of life without the sacrifice of pain and suffering. We think that if we have every comfort available to us, we'll be happy. Too many people think comfort leads to happiness, and if not careful, being comfortable prevents endurance to be built and established. Too many people become disabled by being comfortable, by avoiding struggles in their lives. Some people have lost the adventure of life. We take the elevator, hop in our vehicles, microwave our food, shop online, and it all comes easy, too easy. How many of you have called, texted, or sent an email to a colleague that sits in a desk less than 50 paces away rather than rising to walk into their office for a face-to-face? Some say I might be a bit crazy, but I feel completely ALIVE when I'm pushing and in pain, struggling with discomfort while on the run. I feel ALIVE with the wind blowing in my face, the variety of terrain below my feet, and beads of sweat dripping down my face, burning my eyes. It's through enduring pain and suffering, that I not only feel alive but feel compelled to drive toward the next milestone in my life of leadership.

Welcoming pain and suffering builds endurance. Endurance is necessary to be a high performing leader and without a doubt, endurance is required to live through the demands of life. Given that we all face difficulties and have an inherent fear of failure, we might resist setting daunting goals such as running a marathon. "The marathon" could be any significant challenge you're facing, whether it's the death of a loved one, opening up a business, establishing a lofty team-goal, hiring a risky employee, or battling cancer; we all have fear, and we all have our own "marathons" to face. I believe pain is a milestone towards progress. When we push through it, enduring the struggles and discomfort, we grow. Pushing through the pain can lead to defeating armies far greater, just like the Athenians once did.

To "Lead with Endurance," we welcome challenges and sometimes, we welcome pain and suffering. If we, as leaders, are not willing to be like Pheidippides, enduring whatever "marathon" challenge we face ourselves, how can we possibly lead, influence, and inspire those we lead to endure the struggles they will undoubtedly grapple with? It's easy to be comfortable, but comfort does not lead to growth. Making progress, learning and growing, accomplishing one milestone after the next, brings happiness and pure joy. Through each obstacle, you build endurance and condition yourself to face the next challenge without surrendering as the Persians did.

Since 1987, I have run over 30,000 miles and have never gone much more than six weeks without running. Distance running has taught me valuable lessons, but more importantly, during the countless hours on roads and trails, I have been thinking, reflecting, planning, praying, being grateful, enjoying, slipping, falling, and yes, even crying. Every significant decision I have made, personally and professionally, has been made on a run ... processing every detail, analyzing every perspective, and coming to terms with my decision.

It was not until I surrendered the dream of chasing the sub 4:00 mile, making attempts to qualify for the 1996 and 2000 U.S. Track and Field Olympic Trials, that I finally realized I had already earned the richest prize: an enduring heart and mind. It wasn't long after that I shifted from focusing on race strategies and pursuing personal records, to using my running "think time" to plan for life and career decisions. Some of my best work and decision-making have been accomplished while running on the trails at Hoffmaster State Park, located on the shoreline of Lake Michigan in southern Muskegon County. These wooded dune trails have inspired my greatest ideas for staff meetings, allowed me to recover from the stress of making painful school budget cuts, and helped me mentally craft notes of gratitude to deserving colleagues. Running has sharpened my professional practice, and it has been in mid-stride that I've cultivated some of the best ideas to grow, challenge, and motivate employees. My colleagues would often make fun of my rapid texting or emailing after I completed a run. While the natural endorphins of a "runner's high" certainly boost energy and thinking, it was the uninterrupted time of solitude and reflection that sparked my thoughts.

Sparking thoughts while on a run allowed me to study for exams in college, plan for my engagement proposal to Carrie, my wife of 21 years, think of career pathway decisions, deal with everyday stressors, plan for vacations, develop strategies for parenting three boys, cope with the news of losing a loved one, and a multitude of other vital challenges and opportunities. We endure a lot in the race called life and my running "think time" has allowed me to persevere.

Perseverance is the key to life and leadership. My career has been built on leadership, serving public education for 25 years as a middle school teacher, high school coach, middle school assistant principal, elementary principal, middle school principal, assistant superintendent, and superintendent. Every position I have served has presented a variety of rewards and challenges. As with any career, position, or job, pain and struggling are inevitable. We suffer because we care, and persevering through times of suffering is what separates mediocrity from greatness. Learning how to endure through life and leadership is one of my motivating factors in writing this book. Leadership is not a title. It's a behavior and action that anyone can live. Whether you're an executive for a Fortune 500 company or a volunteer coach on your child's youth soccer team, we all have opportunities to lead. Whether or not we choose to lead, we all live, and it's how we live, and how we endure that can bring pure joy, knowing we reach one milestone after the next, always moving forward!

The Race Plan

Lead with Endurance is divided into two parts:

Part I: The Hurdles

Everyone faces hurdles in life. At multiple times in our lives, we are hit with tragedies or events that are unexpected and difficult to manage. These hurdles help mold us and create the heart of a leader. My hurdles are divided into three chapters.

A Lifetime of Managing Tourette's Syndrome

Conquering a Brain Tumor

Rising Above the Loss of a Highly Public Position

Part II: The Milestones

Why 26.2 milestones?

- Lead with Endurance is a mindset; a will, a drive to succeed, a mission to finish the "race," learning and growing from each milestone along the way.

- Rather than chapters, I have organized *LwE* into milestones with the mindset of not only reaching a certain level but like runners when training, coming back to certain milestones again and again.
- A marathon is 26.2 miles and I experienced the pain, suffering, and joy of completing the Chicago Marathon in October of 2001, just a few weeks after our country endured the terrorist attacks of September 11.
- Seeking treatment options for my brain tumor, I chose radiation as Dr. Fabrizio recommended 26 radiation treatments. Each visit to the Spectrum Cancer Center was a milestone for me, breaking down each visit into steps toward the finish line.

I

THE HURDLES

Enduring Life and Leadership Hurdles

Part I: The Hurdles

Why *Lead with Endurance*? As a runner, my pain has been self-induced, but in life, we have variables that cause pain unexpectedly. It is through the unexpected hurdles that I have grown the most. I have not only strengthened my endurance but have become a better leader because of the challenges. Why? Because enduring is a choice and a mindset.

Lead with Endurance has evolved over time; it has been a process, and after dealing with a lifetime challenge, along with two significant challenges within four years, the voice within told me it was time to share my journey and the variety of "milestones" I have gained along the way.

Conquering Tourette's Syndrome, managing a brain tumor, and grieving the loss of a highly public position has caused significant pain and suffering. Each of these challenges is unique. Dealing with one alone is tough, but combining all three at the same time is very similar to running a marathon, all 26.2 miles. Why connect endurance to leadership? I strongly believe that you have to feel pain and hurt in order to understand and know. Suffering is inevitable as we live and lead. I also believe that you must fail and fall in order to learn and grow. Experiencing loss is a pathway to greater gain. Because many of our life and leadership lessons are learned through pain, I became motivated to write *Lead with Endurance.*

Hurdle 1 - A Lifetime of Managing Tourette's Syndrome

I have Tourette's syndrome, and just like the tics I have endured nearly my entire life, I have chosen to not suppress my fear of acknowledging it publicly. How silly, perhaps cowardly, to not acknowledge, because I know that by simply observing me, eventually, you will know I have tics. When looking in the mirror, I will see an involuntary tic, despite trying to suppress it. Similar to a tic, I feel compelled to release the tension of sharing my lifelong struggles with a syndrome that has presented a lifetime of annoyances. While still a challenge that causes numerous struggles, I am releasing the tension of avoidance in hopes of inspiring and helping others because we must all learn to endure life hurdles.

To this day, the greatest challenge of my life is enduring the social, emotional, and physical pain and suffering of Tourette's syndrome. Tourette syndrome, or TS, is a neurological disorder characterized by repetitive, involuntary movements and vocalizations called tics.

At times, the annoying and uncontrollable tics have caused such intense discomfort in my neck and shoulders that I have had to receive injections to alleviate the pain in my neck. Caused by THOUSANDS of neck muscle contortions each day, the firing of my neck muscles involuntarily and uncontrollably sometimes peak at the rate of 30 - 40 per minute, minute after minute, hour after hour, day after day. During my college years, I persuaded my class advisor to waive a course requirement of taking oral communications because I was too embarrassed to present in front of others. I knew which tics they would see! Just thinking of doing an oral presentation back then caused a flare-up of tics that even impacted how I walked across campus to classes each day.

The early symptoms of TS are typically noticed first in childhood, usually with onset under ten years old. My earliest memories of onset for me, occurred when I was in fourth grade. At times, the firing of eye blinking tics interfered with my reading and concentration in school. Students and even teachers made comments about my tics that left me feeling conscientious and wondering why I couldn't control them. I did not know the root cause, nor did my parents. Throughout middle school, the tics became difficult to manage. When self-esteem and trying to fit in is such a struggle for a "normal" kid, I learned to endure the teasing and comments by making excuses such as telling kids I had something in my eye, or I slept wrong on my neck and was just stretching. Although TS can be a chronic condition with symptoms lasting a lifetime, many people with the condition experience their worst tics in their early teens, with incremental improvement occurring near the end of high school and continuing into adulthood. My tics improved during my high school and college years, but they have remained relatively unchanged since my mid-twenties.

The symptoms of TS are involuntary tics and can only be suppressed, not controlled! The best way I can explain the involuntary tic of TS is comparing a tic to sneezing. You might be able to suppress a sneeze for a short period of time, but eventually, you will sneeze...it will be released!

Tics are classified as either simple or complex. Simple motor tics are sudden, brief, repetitive movements that involve a limited number of muscle groups. Some of the more common simple tics include eye blinking and other eye movements, facial expressions, shoulder shrugging, and head or neck contortions or muscle firing. Simple vocalizations might include repetitive throat-clearing, snorting, sniffing, or grunting sounds. At times, complex motor tics may actually appear purposeful, including sniffing or touching objects, twisting the body, jumping around, flexing, or bending. People coping with TS will often feel or have the desire to complete a tic in a certain way or a certain number of times in order to relieve the urge or decrease the sensation. It cannot be controlled, just suppressed for periods of time. Eventually, the tic will occur! Tics are often worse with stress, anxiety, or excitement, and I have also noticed a heightened increase of tics when I am fatigued and tired. Certain physical experiences can trigger or worsen tics. For example, wearing a necktie may trigger neck tics, which is one of the reasons I prefer to wear a suit or sports jacket without a necktie. Sometimes hearing another person sniff or throat-clear may trigger similar sounds.

Tics wax and wane over time, varying in type, frequency, duration, severity, and location. Although the symptoms of TS are involuntary, some people can sometimes suppress, camouflage, or otherwise manage their tics in an effort to minimize their impact during a specific event or function. However, when this occurs, people with TS report a substantial buildup in "pressure" and tension when suppressing their tics to the point where they feel that the tic must be "released" or expressed, which is one of the most difficult feelings...to do something against your will! On occasion, I will suppress a certain tic as long as possible, perhaps during a highly visible public engagement, but eventually, the tic will need to be released, often retreating to a bathroom or area of privacy. Nowadays, I simply "tic away" without much care or effort to suppress. I am who I am, but it took me years to accept myself and conquer!

Many individuals with TS experience additional neurobehavioral problems that often cause more impairment than the tics themselves. These include inattention, hyperactivity, and impulsivity (attention deficit hyperactivity disorder—ADHD); problems with reading, writing, and arithmetic; and obsessive-compulsive symptoms such as intrusive thoughts/worries and repetitive behaviors. For example, worries about dirt and germs may be associated with repetitive hand-washing. While I do not have a diagnosis of ADHD, those who know me well will tell you that I certainly have the characteristics. My wife will as well! I do face a challenge and history of worrying about germs, displaying obsessive-compulsive disorder, known as OCD. I exhibit behaviors such as frequently carrying small containers of sanitizer in my sports jackets and pockets, using a paper towel to open door handles, and even using sanitizer after every toll both, drive-thru, or exchange of handshaking. I have tried numerous times to relax and not be so obsessive, but like the tics, I have endured and learned to conquer the behavior by developing self coping strategies.

Evidence from twin and family studies suggests that TS is an inherited disorder and that the pattern of inheritance is quite complex. My parents have shared stories about a particular grandparent who demonstrated tics and specific behavior that indicated the evidence of genetics being a factor. Genetic studies also suggest that some forms of ADHD and OCD are genetically related to TS.

Although I denied and wanted to ignore the fact I had TS well into my 30's, it was not until one of my sons demonstrated acute tics for a certain time period, that I accepted my TS. Once realized, it was obvious and incredibly painful for my wife and me to witness. The feelings of guilt became so overwhelming to me, that for the first time in my life, I scheduled an appointment with a professional counselor. As a parent, you do whatever necessary to protect your children from pain and suffering, and I just could not bear that my son would struggle with the same inescapable agony of TS.

Strange enough, my entire career has been in front of people, leading and speaking. Through experiences that tested my grit and resolve: teaching a class of students, coaching a school staff at our weekly meetings, facilitating professional learning for hundreds and even thousands on numerous occasions, I have not only conquered my fear of public speaking, but actually thrive on it. I have conquered TS by going from making excuses and avoiding speaking engagements, to seeking opportunities to speak in front of others.

Conquering TS also has required a lifetime of stretching, massage therapy, chiropractic care, periods of pain medication, and awareness. Just like training for a marathon, dealing with constant tics requires a treatment plan that varies. One of the greatest treatment plans I have is running, where I find myself tic free for extended periods. Running is my reprieve, blessing me with solitude, freedom, and the ability to "run away" from the daily grind of firing muscles that become fatigued and exhausted every tic of the way...

Hurdle 2 - Conquering a Brain Tumor

My first noticeable symptoms started during the winter of 2013. I recognized some hearing loss in my left ear and noticed that sometimes my balance was off as I would brush or bump into a corner when walking quickly at work and at home. I never made the connection that something might be wrong until a close friend of mine, who is a doctor, told me that I needed to get to my family physician and schedule an MRI. Stubbornly, I dismissed the nudge and did not make an appointment. A month later that same friend, Chad Uptigrove, stated in no uncertain terms that if I continued to neglect my serious symptoms, he would make the appointments for me. His eyes were flooded with concern and his voice terse with exasperation. The symptoms had become exacerbated, so I scheduled an appointment with my family physician.

Leading up to a spring break trip in 2014, I had an MRI scheduled. New symptoms began to present themselves, such as tingling sensations in my face and in other areas of my body. I became hypersensitive to the feelings in my body and my own anxiety caused the symptoms to intensify. Departing for our family spring break to Branson, Missouri was supposed to be filled with joyful expectation, but I was plagued with worry and a heavy heart. Additional pressure mounted, as I knew that the Board of Education would soon be acting on a recommendation to move me into an Assistant Superintendent position with a long-term objective of developing a succession plan for me to become the next Superintendent of Mona Shores Public Schools, Norton Shores, Michigan.

The comfort in this trip was that I would be with my family; my wife and our three sons, Hayden, Jackson, and Landon, and we would be traveling with our great friends and neighbors, the Uptigrove Family. Dr. Chad Uptigrove, D.O., is not only a wonderful friend of mine, but he is also a highly respected family physician and provides training and tutelage for residents in the West Michigan area. I was grateful for this time with my friend and confidant to help me process the dramatic heightening of symptoms that I was now experiencing. Quite honestly, without Chad, I would have canceled the vacation, but I knew our family truly needed this time away.

During this time away, I realized the magnitude and source of my stress: some of my symptoms were directly caused by the alarm of being referred to a neurologist for the troubling balance and tingling issues, but these concerns were compounded by the upcoming succession plan for my rise to a highly public position. My hearing loss and balance issues were now believed to be the result of something else occurring in my brain, and this ignited turmoil and racing fears like never before. It made sense when my neurologist, Dr. Ivan Landan, M.D., pronounced, "You clearly have two issues that we need to treat and sort out. Treat the anxiety first, then we will focus on the other symptoms." After mentally accepting the mounting obstacles ahead: an upcoming MRI test and the career ascension to a highly public position, I began to calm, respecting my limited control over these circumstances. After all, I was a tough-minded person and a distance runner who not only endured pain regularly but valued it like a badge of honor.

Vividly, I remember that my MRI was scheduled on a Friday evening, and we had dinner plans with the Uptigrove Family. Being strapped onto the table without movement and being conveyed into a narrow tube was not fun for a highly energetic, never-sit-still person. What caught my attention was when the technician told me they needed to inject me with dye to do some additional testing, which was not initially explained to me. While I am far from a physician, I pressed the technician quite candidly and rather aggressively about the need for this, but no deviation from protocol was permitted. Experienced educators develop skills for reading people, and there was no doubt the technician knew the severity of my pending diagnosis. Why the injection of dye? Something was terribly wrong.

Returning home, I found the Uptigrove Family seated around our table, and I candidly divulged my experience and questioned the dye being injected. My question resonated with Chad; as a physician, he knew immediately that something suspicious had been found during the scan. On that night, however, surrounded by both of our families, Chad did the right thing and harbored his thoughts as we laughed, played board games, and later sipped wine with our wives around a cozy fire in our great room. Though the food and drinks were sumptuous and the companionship unmatched, I was in silent terror. The tingling in my body continued, and now more than ever I was acutely aware of every threatening sensation. That night, after the Uptigroves departed, I stole down to the basement and wept - desperately praying for God's guidance and mercy. Carrie and the boys should not have to shoulder these fears, and I resolved to spare them of this anguish for as long as I could.

A few days later while I was at work, I received a phone call from my family physician. Why was my doctor, not the nurse, calling with results? My breaths came in jagged gasps as my heart raced. Dr. Brennan asked, "Greg, are you sitting down?" While I immediately knew the MRI results must have revealed something concerning, I was not prepared for Dr. Brennan's next words. "Greg, I wanted to personally contact you. I am sorry to share that your MRI results show a brain tumor. While uncertain of the type, it appears we caught the tumor early. I would like you to visit with a neurosurgeon and begin learning about what options you will have for treatment."

Waves of shock rippled through my body. Seconds after hanging up the phone, Mr. Wahlberg, an 8th-grade science teacher, entered my office to ask me a few questions about a new course I was persuading him to teach the following year. As a leader, you learn how to quickly shift from one conversation to the next without hesitation. Following my conversation with Mr. Wahlberg, I transitioned to our conference room for a bi-weekly meeting with our Operations Director, custodial management team, assistant principals, day-time custodian, and secretary. I walked into my next meeting wondering how I was going to share this news with my wife. As always, I facilitated the meeting trying to not let the recent news impact my performance in a negative way. As a leader, it doesn't matter what kind of day you're having at home or in the office, the next individual or group deserves your best, enduring the focus and concentration of the next task at hand.

Enduring two back-to-back meetings after the shocking news from Dr. Brennan, I closed my door in my office and it hit me...I have a brain tumor. Strangely, I could not keep my thoughts from shifting to the worst-case scenario. Sitting at my desk, I thought of my own death. Before leaving the office, I collected myself and walked down to the sixth-grade hallway. My oldest son, Hayden, was a sixth-grade student in the building, and I was just Hayden's dad walking into his classroom, not the middle school principal. I needed to see Hayden and be comforted by his thousand-watt smile. Little did Hayden's teacher know, I was not interested in her teaching, nor how she was managing her classroom. I was only there because I simply needed to see my son. It grounded me to see Hayden, but I also left the classroom holding back tears of the unknown. What kind of tumor was growing in my brain? As I left the office that night, I cried all the way home. Carrie met me at the door and we held each other in a heartbreaking hug. It was a long cry, but I could not show my emotions around the boys. After all, Hayden had just seen me in his classroom earlier in the day and everything was normal. Collecting myself, I headed downstairs to greet the boys as "dad" - a perpetual figure of strength and playfulness. They had no glimmer of the terror and grief that was shattering me inside.

A restless night of panic followed. Not wanting to wake Carrie, I found my way downstairs. In the lonely quiet, I did not mourn but began planning for the worst-case scenario. Not knowing the type of brain tumor, whether it was malignant or benign, my thoughts became consumed by how I could prepare my family and the school district if I became deathly ill, unable to be successfully treated. The alarming tingling sensations continued and my mind raced. However, I needed to be strong both at home and at work. I cherished the great many who counted on me. I needed to endure. What would be the next milestone?

With Dr. Brennan and Dr. Uptigrove, Carrie and I began researching and consulting with multiple experts in the medical field, including neurosurgeons and experts around the country. We finally visited the Spectrum Health Cancer Center at Lemmen-Holton Cancer Pavilion, located in the medical mile of Grand Rapids, MI. After additional MRI's and a treatment plan with treatment options, it was not until I met Dr. Fabrizio, Radiation Oncologist, that I became comforted. In an empathetic tone and gesture, Dr. Fabrizio leaned toward Carrie and me to present his three treatment options. In a calm, confident voice, my heart grabbed ahold of his words, "Greg, unless we do brain surgery and take a biopsy, we will not be 100% certain of the type of tumor we're facing. You understand the risks with surgery and the risks with radiation. One option is 26 treatments of radiation..." I didn't hear anything after I heard 26. Perhaps it was Dr. Fabrizio's calm, confident voice tone. Some might call it irony or divine intervention, but I am confident God was speaking to me when Dr. Fabrizio mentioned 26 rounds of radiation. As a runner, I quickly grabbed ahold of 26 - the distance of a marathon - and I knew that while it might be challenging, I could endure. Carrie and I confirmed the treatment plan of 26 rounds of radiation, and I left prepared to begin the next race.

Preparing for my radiation treatments, I not only felt comforted by my confidence in a successful plan, but I was also comfortable knowing I had a treatment plan that I could break down into a "race plan," similar to the Chicago Marathon. The first step was a return trip to Spectrum Health Cancer Center to be fitted for a treatment mask, a mold of my face that would be buttoned-down, secured during the radiation treatment to eliminate movement.

While I know mindset is critical to enduring the pain and suffering of running a marathon, I did not want to burden my family, friends, and colleagues; therefore, Carrie and I remained very selective in our trust of sharing such sensitive information. Not only did I not want to burden people, but I was also working in a highly public position, and our Board of Education had just made a motion to move me into the Assistant Superintendent Position with a succession plan to become the next Superintendent. My first radiation treatment was scheduled for May 15th, and while I was finishing up my final weeks as the Principal at

Mona Shores Middle School, I refused to allow my tumor and treatment to impact my performance in a negative way. My goal was to depart from Mona Shores Middle School as a strong leader, fully engaged, just as I had entered the building five years previous. I wanted to give the staff and students a memorable finish to what had been an incredible journey of transforming the culture at MSMS. At the time, I only shared my diagnosis and treatment plans with the two assistant principals and the lead secretary. I knew I could count on them to help me finish one race strong and begin my next race with a great start. I also needed the three of them to understand why I might be missing some work as it was rare that I missed a day.

My pre-race plan for treatment consisted of beginning with the end in mind. I knew that my final treatment would be on July 7th and I wanted to have a celebratory pool party with family and close friends to "Dunk the Tumor" and later after our guests departed, burn the plastic face mask that would be used to restrict my head during radiation treatment. July 7th was the finish line for my treatment. I knew, based on running a marathon, I would need to incrementally break down the treatments into milestones, smaller goals of success, such as reaching the halfway point, checking off each milestone along the way. I also knew that I could not do this race alone, and I am thankful for my family that divided up treatment sessions with me just in time to give me some needed relief and support when traveling to Grand Rapids from Muskegon each day. I was ready to begin the race of my life!

What I didn't realize is how restrictive the mask would feel and how claustrophobic the radiation machine would be. I also knew that I would have to overcome the feeling of being isolated and having my head secured to the treatment table, tightly buttoned down for 8-12 minutes each session. I refused to become sedated for each treatment because I did not want to burden my family with making the commute to every treatment, and I would often return to work after each treatment. I adjusted my race plan. Before each treatment, I grabbed an eight-ounce cup of cold water with crushed ice, visualized my tumor shrinking, said a prayer, took deep breaths to relax and repeated with each treatment, so I could break down each treatment into a smaller race. After five treatments, I knew I could endure without receiving sedation, and I continued with the same mental relaxation, prayer, and self-talk for every radiation treatment to follow. With practice and acute focus, by the 8th treatment, I found a routine that became incredibly meditative and relaxing, completely ignoring the distractions around me. Every session included a mindset of gratitude and positive thoughts about my wife, boys, scripture from my mom, and a transition plan of my focus at work.

About halfway through the course of treatments, I woke up in the middle of the night and could not stop thinking about my treatment and wondering, what if it didn't work? What if the tumor was malignant? With my mind racing once again, I did not want to wake Carrie, so I began to head to the basement to sleep. The tears started to flow. What was this feeling? I was incredibly confident about the treatment plan. Halfway through treatments, I knew I needed to refocus. I did not want my three boys and wife to see me so vulnerable, and I knew that the finish line was on the downside. On the way back from the 13th treatment, my dad had said, "It's downhill from here son, the finish line will be in sight very soon. We will dunk the tumor on July 7th. Stay focused and let me know if you want me to be with you for every treatment from here forward." It was always nice to have my dad join me as he did, but I also had work to do and spending time on the phone while traveling back and forth to Grand Rapids provided a great opportunity to work, return messages, and make phone calls without interruptions. Whether my dad joined me or not, I knew my dad's powerful mindset was with me and his confidence provided me strength. As with the many races I competed in over the years, my dad would see me at the finish line. Finishing radiation treatments would be no different!

After school was out for the summer, Carrie and the boys wanted to join me for a treatment session. I completed my routine, grabbed a cup of water with shaved ice, said my prayers, visualized my tumor shrinking, and gave myself a pep-talk. But this would be different as I wanted Carrie and the boys to see the mask, and see me strapped into the radiation machine, knowing that this could be a life lesson for my boys on how to be resilient, develop stamina, and endure challenges in life. After I was secure, Carrie and the boys were escorted out, as only the patient is allowed while radiation is being administered. As they were leaving, not able to see them because of the tight restrictions of the mask, I reached through the tiny enclosure to give each boy a fist bump. With each fist bump, I could easily tell who it was by their touch and finally, the comforting three-hand squeeze by Carrie...three squeezes for "I... Love... You," a squeeze that we do when holding hands. I remember my prayer was different that day...I prayed that none of my family members would have to deal with such treatment. But if they did, I prayed that they would be able to endure. Life is tough, leadership can be rough. For some reason, the treatment did not seem as long that day, knowing my family was waiting. I wanted to lead my family through this race with an attitude of endurance, toughness, faith, grace, resilience, and gratitude.

Besides telling my three colleagues at the middle school about my brain tumor, I told my direct report, the Superintendent at the time, and also our Human Resource Director. I told both of them before my treatments started, and I will not forget our HR Director asking me how I was managing everything because she noticed I had made the transition into the central office with an energy unknown and an organization that she had not ever seen. She told me she was amazed at how I was able to work 10-12 hours a day and couldn't believe the leadership I had already brought to the central office and my official start date had yet to begin. I had been feeling like I would not be able to fully focus on the transition as intended because of the tremendous distraction, I was facing personally. However, at that point, I knew I would be just fine in my new role, and the succession plan with my transition to the superintendent was progressing forward.

Feeling confident in my treatment plan that was nearing an end and excited about the impact and gains I was making in my new leadership position, I was able to shift my mind from another negative reality to a positive. Due to the growth of the tumor and the radiation treatments, another milestone came into the picture. Because of the location of the tumor, I experienced hearing loss due to damage to the nerve pathways from the brain to the inner ear. On the upswing, although difficult to accept that my left ear would have permanent hearing loss, I was able to turn the hearing loss into a positive...it's all about the mindset. Near our backyard, we have a pond, and when the water and air temps hit a certain temperature after a long Michigan winter, the frogs begin to make their harmony. Our family always looks forward to the day we hear our first peep. The joys of hearing the spring peepers eventually become a distraction to sleep because they peep all night long. During the peak of the mating season, the peeping becomes more like a constant buzz of high-frequency annoyances, waking you up throughout the night. Moving forward, I can enjoy the welcoming sound of spring at any time, and by simply turning onto my pillow with my left ear up, I don't hear a peep. I now look forward to every spring even more!

Mindset is everything...it allows you to endure!

With just a few milestones left, I was looking forward to the upcoming July 4th holiday as my sister and her family would be joining us, and she would be attending the 25th milestone of treatment. On the final treatment, it was a strange feeling, similar to finishing a long race. I was excited about seeing the finish line but also felt grateful for the journey that had just occurred. Yes, grateful for radiation blasting the tumor in my brain. I was grateful that I had endured 26 milestones of treatment while finishing my work at the middle school and providing a smooth, seamless transition with my successor who would eventually do the job much better than I did. I was able to transition to the central office and bring some organization and structure with curriculum and assessment plans, begin the foundation of a strategic plan, restructure our district leadership team meeting schedule, overhaul the evaluation system for administrators and teachers, and assist with contract negotiations with our teaching staff. More importantly, I was able to endure radiation treatments without burdening my children and wife, doing my best to protect them from seeing me vulnerable, so they could finish the end of their school year without being distracted.

Hurdle 3 - Rising Above the Loss of a Highly Public Position

The voice on the line said, "A formal, written complaint has been filed against you for alleged acts of bullying and harassment the past two and a half years." I could not utter a word in response. Shock and confusion pulsed through me in a baffled wave. Never, personally or professionally, had I been accused of being someone who harasses or bullies. From that sickening moment to the months following my resignation, I experienced unfathomable shock, disbelief, and disgust at the contrived scheme for my ruination. Because of the genuine passion I had for the organization, the people I served, and the results we were achieving with a highly performing administrative team, the thoughts of turning over the role to someone else was incomprehensible. Because of the publicity of my position as superintendent and a new influx of media attention, I now faced another distressing challenge in my life. November 14, 2017: exploited by an unfortunate timeline of events and what appeared to be highly-orchestrated collusion, I was railroaded into resigning from my beloved position as superintendent. Personally and professionally, I was suffering! Another race to endure...

My letter of resignation stated (Jointly agreed upon with Board of Education):

November 14, 2017

Dear Board of Education,

Sometimes the best thing a leader can do is step away and turn over the role to someone else. The issues that have manifested the past 9 months have become a major distraction to our most important focus; improving teaching and learning, inspiring excellence, building character and impacting the future through academics, arts, and athletics.

With a heavy heart, please accept this letter as my resignation from Superintendent, effective November 14, 2017. I am grateful for the opportunity of serving the past nine years, serving as your Middle School Principal, Assistant Superintendent, and most recently Superintendent.

I was honored when the Board of Education asked me to serve as Assistant Superintendent while developing a succession plan to become the next Superintendent. Thank you for allowing me to serve in three roles that have brought me a tremendous amount of gratitude, learning, and growth. Together, we were able to accomplish a significant portion of our District Strategic Plan due to the great leaders and educators we have in our district.

Because of our District Strategic Plan, we improved teaching and learning by refining our common curricular alignment in a variety of content areas and grade levels and implemented blended learning environments throughout the District. We have improved our relationships and communication by using skillful and timely feedback, and by using technology and social media as an ongoing tool for effective, transparent communication at all levels within the school community. Finally, in regards to facilities and finances,

21

we were able to renew our sinking fund, successfully pass a millage increase, and negotiate successful employee contracts while meeting our fund balance goals. I am grateful to the people who helped us achieve these goals. It is one of the reasons I love this district and the people who work here.

Much more important than the roles I served, I have gained the utmost respect for our community, and the relationships that have been formulated with all of our stakeholders. I am thankful for the Board of Education, our District Leadership Team (Administrators), our staff and faculty, parents, and students. This district is special because of the people and it was an honor to work with everyone.

Moving forward, I wish everyone well. As I remain a community member, please know that I will continue to do anything to move this district forward, if ever needed.

Sailing forward,

Greg Helmer

Even though it was believed the complainant's original complaints of harassment and bullying for two-and-a-half years were not substantiated, I was not running away from my responsibilities. However, to move forward as a healthy organization, I told members of the Board of Education that I needed to go, the complainant needed to go, or we both needed to go. The only variable I could control was that I go. Throughout my entire life, I have been running toward something, moving forward, sometimes suffering, yet always driving towards the finish line. This time, while I was not running away, I did not know exactly where or what I would be running to. The next milestone was unclear.

Falling down doesn't make someone a failure; staying down does. After nine months of a significant distraction to my personal and professional life, it was time to surrender. I hate quitting, but it was clear, due to compiling complaints of retaliation by the complainant against me, I was hamstrung. After being placed on a paid administrative leave of absence, I immediately began to mourn in a way that I had never experienced in my life. The suffering was intense. For 72 hours, the grieving was painful - painful because my heart was broken, painful because I felt I had let my family, friends, administrative team, the board of education, and the school community down. The damage seemed insurmountable. My distinguished and impeccable 24-year career was unjustly tarnished. My tremendous work for a district I loved with my whole heart was utterly forsaken. I had made the right but the difficult and painful decision on behalf of the community, and now the ones I loved most dearly, my wife and children, would suffer for it. As a leader, if you stick around long enough, you will experience pain and suffering, even when behaving and leading with the greatest of intentions.

During the intense days of mourning, I became emotionally, mentally, and physically drained. Despite the steady consumption of water and flood of support by family, friends, and colleagues, constant tears and stress left me weak and dehydrated. The pain was much more intense than any moment during the initial news and treatment of my brain tumor. The sharp suffering reminded me of those excruciating last miles completing the Chicago Marathon. Even though 16 years had passed, I thought back to that marathon on numerous occasions during the grieving process of losing my position as superintendent. At times, my tears and crying were uncontrollable, and it was difficult because the mourning included many of my loved ones as well. To see my family, friends, colleagues, and community members hurt, deepened my pain. But to see my own wife and children grieve, was simply raw and unbearable at times. Unlike the brain tumor, resigning from my position as superintendent was much more intense, simply because as leaders, we impact so many lives, and for me, I felt that I lost a fight that would not help the organization move forward, but regress. While devastating and uncertain for me, I refused to violate my core values or settle for mediocrity from those for whom I am responsible. I could not allow the debilitation and drama to continue, even if it cost me my job! It was painful because it seemed that dirty politics had interfered with my ability to hold certain people accountable. Many others knew as well, but they caved when the pressure was on. To do what is easy, or to do what is right?

Particularly insufferable was that my wife, Carrie, had to experience the turmoil and heartbreak right alongside me. To make the emotions even more complex, Carrie had taught mathematics at our high school for 24 years and was the math department chair. One of her direct supervisors was not only the administrator who filed harassment, bullying, and eventually retaliation claims against me but had also refused to speak with my wife since the complaints were filed. All three of our boys attended school in this district. Carrie and I were in deep mourning together. We could not eat. Holding each other and comforting each other was the only thing we could do that felt good, felt helpful. The cycle of tears and uncontrollable shaking occurred endlessly. Carrie told me that on two occasions, I cried in my sleep, which only caused her more pain, knowing I was literally crying in my sleep. While we did manage to get some sleep days after my resignation, we never seemed to feel rested until months later.

After several days of intense mourning, I finally forced my mind to think of moving forward. Although the first 72 hours following my resignation felt more painful than the marathon, I knew that just like the marathon, I would heal, recover, and move forward, even if moving forward meant a shuffle at first. The confusion and difficulty for me were that I had always thrived on following a plan. My life and career have always been built on having a detailed plan. I had draft plans of leadership meetings arranged months and in some cases, a full year in advance. Everything I did was calculated and purposeful. Over my career, I moved from one leadership position to another seamlessly and deliberately, knowing and planning ahead for a smooth departure and entrance into each career path.

There was nothing smooth about being personally escorted from a conference room by the Board of Education's attorney to my office. There was nothing smooth when my wife entered my office and asked what was going on, and I had to explain that I was being placed on paid administrative leave, and had agreed to work on a severance agreement to depart from my job. My time as the superintendent was over. My wife was not familiar with me surrendering, but I felt my leadership was hindered due to the current constraints. Our lives would change forever, and for the first time, we both felt like our lives were out of control.

We do not control everything. The minute we think we do, we will be reminded that life is tough and leadership is rough. We looked at refinancing or selling our house, moving to a different location to get a jumpstart on my next career position, we revamped our household budget, and tightened down on our spending. Stripped of my livelihood, we felt our comfort and security threatened. What of the family dream home Carrie and I had built in 2004? We had purposefully chosen that idyllic neighborhood, as it is just minutes from schools for our boys and running distance to Lake Michigan and PJ Hoffmaster State Park – places that our family visited often and places I built my personal and professional endurance, milestone after milestone.

The trails of PJ Hoffmaster are ingrained in my heart and soul. For more than thirty years, the park has been my place of solace and resurgence. I have traveled thousands of miles in these dunes: sometimes testing my physical limits racing up a woodland rise and sometimes just striding easily along a shoreline trail overlooking one of the world's largest freshwater lakes. Always, I emerge from the trails aglow with both inspiration and contentment. It was on a particular run, coincidently 26 days after resigning as the superintendent, that I became awash with a deep sense of peace about my future and a strong feeling of pride for what I'd endured. My resignation was difficult, but it was right. As my dad always said, "At the beginning of the day and at the end of the day, you should look yourself in the mirror, knowing what you will do or what you have done is right." On that night the reflection showed a man who was once broken but now possessed a fiery new passion for whatever race came next. How and where would my leadership impact the next organization? How and who would I help endure their own personal and professional races?

Before rising above the loss of a highly public position, I needed answers. Most of my answers eventually emerged, but some totally surprised me even weeks and months after I resigned. I was told that I was naive to the collusion that had occurred, but it was too late to react. Frankly, I am stunned by how someone can thrive on deceit and lead a movement bent on dismantling what is sound and just. I was told the complainant believed I was provoking their exit, but I was solely focused on their growth as a leader and stakeholder and endeavored to coach this administrator like the hundreds of employees I'd led for 18 years as a school administrator. Before thinking further about the future, my mind needed to effectively assess the fiasco that had just occurred. I didn't have many answers as questions were coming my way, which only confirmed what was believed to be deceit, lies, and self-centered thinking of a small group who were apparently in cahoots to take me down, working through a "secret club" that became much clearer when I read an email written by a former consultant. I became privy to the communication when a highly respected school leader called me and said, "I am sending you an email. It clearly explains what was going on behind your back. Greg, you were framed!"

The following day after my resignation, the consultant sent a communication to a wide spread audience, including Bcc: recipients that mentioned the following:

- An announcement of my resignation written in a "celebratory" fashion
- The mention of changing Board Policy 1662, which is the district's anti-harassment policy
- Thanking the group for listening, offering advice and support the past 2 ½ years as "we moved this work forward one inch at a time"

When I read this email for the first time, I was shocked and sickened. Strangely, the devastation was mitigated knowing there was a "we" behind this bogus scheme. Their toxic machination had brought my career to a crossroads, and it would impact my entire family in a variety of ways. I was baffled by how leading so purposefully and truthfully could inspire such a vicious, politically driven plan by such a small resentful group. Despite the challenge, I knew that I would find a way to put one foot in front of the other, just as I did while training as a distance runner, moving toward the next milestone. Realizing that the public and so many people within our district and community would never know the truth because of the separation agreement and my choice to not have a hearing open to the public, I needed to make sense of the unsensible. As a leader I have never shrunk from daunting challenges, but rather I have found the greatest organizational progress made when analyzing the brutal facts, by providing candid feedback for improvement, and holding those I manage and lead accountable to be their best. In doing so, I have never wavered from my standard of protecting the dignity of those I lead and respecting their skills and talents, and now I needed the raw truth. How did I become railroaded by such evilness?

I now faced a "race" that I had not registered for and for which I had no training plan in place. I didn't even know the distance of this particular race, nor could I see the finish line. What I did know was that my leadership in this position was finished. My career pathway would be rerouted onto new terrain, and my endurance would be challenged like never before. Failure is part of life and leadership, and debacles are inevitable. Major failures are difficult to endure, but endure we must! Searing shame and embarrassment accompany failure. Our hindsight becomes a weight crashing down, obliterating our pride. We think we should have known better and done better. Because of my highly public position, my entire family felt the feeling of failure and humiliation, and this was a perfect story for the press and media to obtain reader attention.

But with the right mindset and drive, failure can be and should be a significant part of our success story, so the sooner we quit feeling sorry for ourselves, the better off we will be in utilizing the lessons of growth and seizing the new opportunities in front of us! Before I could pick myself up, and stop feeling sorry for myself, I needed to know how I had fallen. Standing on the shoreline of Lake Michigan, suffering during the middle of a run, more like a shuffle because of emotional exhaustion, I stopped and asked, "What the hell just happened?".

My story in its entirety cannot be told as some details and facts remain undisclosed. As stated in my separation agreement and release:

"Whereas, the District and Helmer are entering this Agreement, with full knowledge of their respective rights and of the provisions hereof, without any admission of fault, wrongdoing, or liability on the part of either party."

Interestingly enough, the Board of Education released a forty-seven page investigative summary report for bullying and harassment complaints against me; however, the official investigative report, which is several hundred pages, remains protected and privileged. My attorney wanted to make the entire investigation public, but in the days ahead, we decided litigation and going public was not in my heart or will. Assessing the fiasco, I unfolded the timeline of suspicious events and circumstances. After the fallout, I learned even more about the claims of collusion, framing, and organized attack on my position and mission to hold certain people accountable.

I remember during a Board of Education meeting on November 6, 2017, a community member asked the school board a question about why Board Policy 1662 had been revised just two weeks before the accusations came out against me. I just about fell out of my seat, because this was certainly a factor that played in the evilness. The community member realized that on February of 2017, the Board of Education adopted a revision to the anti-harassment policy, stating:

If a Complainant informs the Board President, either orally or in writing, about any complaint of harassment or retaliation by the Superintendent, the Board President must report such information to the District's attorney within two (2) business days, and the District's attorney will act as the Compliance Officer's designee.

The significant revision transferred the responsibility of the Complainant to the Board President. Following the board meeting, a few of the district administrators shared their concern as it appeared the role and responsibility of our Board President were being altered by someone going rogue!

My struggles seemed to have all started by making attempts to coach, grow, and hold a long-standing administrator accountable once I obtained an authority position over this person and became their direct report, supervisor and evaluator. Throughout the summer of 2017, many trusted colleagues continued to share opinions of dirty politics and how certain forces interfered with my ability to do my job. I became hamstrung and unable to perform my job duties when a "Plan of assistance" stipulation removed me from supervising and evaluating this administrator. I was told the stipulation was provided to protect me, the District, and the complainant. Doing the right thing, unfortunately in this case, allowed for politics to totally destroy what was a high performing, highly synergistic district leadership team. I had hired, or been involved with either hiring or promoting the vast majority of the administrators on our district leadership team. Ironically, three positions I was not involved with were from...you got it, the complainant's building. It's unfortunate that certain people could not endure when the pressure was on and difficult decisions needed to be made.

Just two weeks after I resigned, at a state level administrative conference, a breakout session being facilitated by an educational consultant titled, "Adult Bullying in the Schoolhouse" was on the schedule. On poster paper, "Our district's name...Policy 1662" was written. The session was attended by an administrator from our district not recognized by the consultant...the same consultant who was befriended by the complainant.

Posted in the program, the session was described with the following objectives:

- Helping practicing principals understand the impact of bullying
- Understanding the impact of bullying on the school culture when involving adults
- Learning strategies for providing specific feedback to those who initiate bullying behavior
- Assisting those in need who need to stay strong when dealing with bullying
- Focusing on relational aggression within the context of women in the workplace

Before the session ended, it was reported to me that the administrator from our district left the room, disgusted and appalled by what was heard.

Between my resignation and shortly after the statewide annual conference, so many questions came my way, but I didn't have the answers. Questions have been asked such as...Why would this particular consultant indirectly refer to me and my resignation at a statewide conference? Why would the consultant, who was once considered a friend and colleague, do such a thing? Why would this consultant, someone who asked me to present with her at multiple state conferences, someone who asked me to speak to her own graduate students, someone I once considered a friend, do such a thing? Was it because the consultant earned nearly $80,000 from our district as a part-time consultant and coach, and I terminated services when I became the superintendent? Was it because after terminating services, the consultant continued to coach one specific administrator who happen to file a bullying and harassment complaint against me? Why would the consultant contact the executive coach assigned by the Board of Education to coach me, and ask my coach such confidential, unprofessional and unethical questions? How would the consultant even know who my hired coach was when only the Board of Education and I were privy? Could it be someone going rogue, again, working behind the scenes? Why would a board member ask for "off the record" meetings with direct reports to me and call a previous district to inquire about how someone felt about my leadership when I left the former district eight years prior? Why would this board member rate my end of the year evaluation with scores that were not reflective of the entire board, and in many areas, glaringly opposite and contradictory? Despite what would've been a very fair and objective evaluation process, my end of the year rating was "effective." Regardless of who and why, evilness lurked again...too many questions by reliable credible leaders. Perhaps resigning would make me feel free?

Several months after I resigned, I was asked multiple questions I could not answer. During a time I was trying to forget about the fiasco and move forward with new leadership projects, my response to most of the questions remained the same. I didn't know and I couldn't imagine. I have been asked if I knew about the complainant and a small group of friends organizing a "book club" to take me down, perhaps the same group that the educational consultant references as "we" in her email communication. I just don't know, and if so, I couldn't imagine.

What I do know is that I came into the District in 2009 and joined an administrative team that was well established, but mediocre at best in regards to overall leadership and synergy as a team. Isolation was evident, and trust was fractured because of a lack of focus on team dynamics and common goals. The administrative team lacked instructional leadership. After sharing my opinion and thoughts on a few topics up front, I sensed that central office was closed-minded to new ideas. I quickly learned the source of dysfunction for this leadership team. My paramount priority would be to transform the culture at the middle school as their new principal, because the administrative team, at that time, seemed to be controlled by a long-standing building level principal who had far too much power and latitude for such a position, and a culture within the administrative team that blindly and ignorantly accepted all terms from central office without questioning what was best practice and what was right.

But I was accustomed to questioning throughout my entire career, so I questioned and spoke, and over time, an undeniable shift in the pecking order of our administrative team developed. What was strange is that our long-time employee and experienced administrator on the team (the complainant), did not seem to have any real or substantive relationships with many other administrators on the team. I quickly grew to love, respect, and enjoy learning with my new colleagues. While relationships grew and strengthened, it was noticeable that one of our colleagues continued to isolate themselves from the team.

When the new superintendent was hired during the summer of 2011, this same administrator continued to share her frustrations, disgust, and negativity about the Board's choice. I thought the new superintendent had the perfect skill set for the needs of the district and I quickly grew fond of our new leader. I appreciated that he was real, authentic, and valued him for his ability to heal the district following a ponzi scheme. He was not fake!

My relationship with this administrator continued to diminish. I made several attempts to connect, collaborate, and sought opportunities to develop a relationship, but this administrator remained distant and lacked confidence. She never made me feel welcomed. Prior to being hired in the district, during the summer of 2009, I reached out to her when I was researching and looking into whether or not I should apply for the middle school principal position, she was standoffish. I only knew her through my wife because she was her boss, and had attended a few workshops in the county as participants over the years. We were only acquaintances. I remember vividly, when she told me it would be a daunting task to take on the armpit of the District. She was quick to explain how the culture was toxic, and would be an exhausting job for anyone. She told me I should run away from such a position.

Her words were nothing new from what I was hearing, but it would seem that she would be more encouraging and enthusiastic about the great opportunity...little did I know, eight years later, I was told the same administrator wanted me to run away for good.

II

THE MILESTONES

26.2 Milestones for Improving Life and Leadership

Part II: The Milestones

Introduction:

Do you lead others? Whether you're a parent leading your family or children, serving as a volunteer coach on your child's youth club sport team, owner of a small company, leading a church, managing a department or region, a teacher in a classroom, a coach of a middle school or high school team, leading a school or district as an educational leader, serving on a board of trustees, or hired as CEO, I am convinced, if applied, the 26.2 Leadership/Life Milestones will provide you insight and tools to learn, grow, and ultimately become a better leader to those you serve.

Leadership requires endurance. Leading people and working with people requires constant stamina. I have been a competitive runner since 1987, the beginning of my sophomore year at Orchard View High School, located in Muskegon, MI. While on the trails of Hoffmaster State Park, along the shoreline of Lake Michigan, and the miles or roads all around West Michigan, I have learned how enduring the hardships and experiencing the highlights of running directly connect to leadership and life. For the past 25 years, my professional career has been focused on educational leadership, serving in roles as a middle school teacher, high school coach, middle school assistant principal,

elementary principal, middle school principal, assistant superintendent, and superintendent. Eighteen years of educational leadership in
a variety of administrative positions have been incredibly rewarding,
while leading, supporting, and influencing some of the best educators,
teachers, and school communities in West Michigan. Every position
has been my favorite until the next one comes along. While each
organization and building is different, one thing is certain...endurance
is essential for the health of any club, business, group, or organization.
A leader without the tenacity to endure pain, struggles, and hardships,
will not cross the finish line successfully!

Why Lead with Endurance (LwE)? Over my career I have developed my
professional endurance by focusing on milestones, which include (3LQ)
Listen, Look, Learn, and Question. 3LQ has simply been a mindset of
thinking that I have personally developed into my leadership style of
how I act, think, and ultimately lead.

Over the past several years, my running thoughts have shifted from
thinking about how to improve my time, beat the competition, advance
to the next interval workout, or develop a plan for the next race, to
thinking about leadership and my work at hand.

As leaders, one of our greatest challenges is leading ourselves, facing
milestones and enduring the obstacles that confront us, personally and
professionally. How might we expect to take others farther than we have
pushed or challenged ourselves? We must endure within before we can
lead, influence, and impact those we serve. It is known that numerous
high performing leaders have surrendered far short of their potential
because they were not able to endure the pain and suffering. Too often,
highly skilled leaders seek the glory and fulfillment of crossing a finish
line in leadership only to discover that it's the journey of enduring that

completed the race of leadership. There are no shortcuts to the finish line. Ultimately, it's each milestone between the start and finishes that give us the glory, a glory in knowing we have the character, mindset, and drive to not only accept challenges but welcome the fear of questioning whether or not we will endure.

I have learned that everything worthwhile in life and leadership is like a marathon. According to John Maxwell, "There is a truth you need to recognize, not just for leadership, but for everything in life. Everything worthwhile is uphill. The word everything is inclusive. It's all-encompassing. Pair that with worthwhile - the things that are desirable, appropriate, good for you, attractive, beneficial. So when you think about that, it's very significant. Anything and everything you desire in life, everything you would like to strive for, is uphill, meaning the pursuit of it is challenging, grueling, exhausting, strenuous, and difficult."

Success does not come by chance. No person has completed a marathon without knowing how they were able to reach 26.2 milestones from start to finish, pushing through the obstacles not only on race day but the months and sometimes years of training. It's the effort that matters. Maxwell continues, "No leader who ever led people to do something significant did it without great effort. Any climb uphill must be deliberate, consistent, and willful. It is very intentional." Everything worthwhile is uphill, like a marathon, not only describes life and leadership but provides rationale on how the mindset and drive are so essential for enduring whatever challenge you perceive as your "marathon."

When running any long-distance race, the goal is not to beat others, as you might in a 100 meter-dash. Instead, the focus is to endure your own race - to achieve your own personal milestones. Whether other people finish in front of or behind you, it is only because their personal milestones are more or less than yours. May the wind be at your back, and the learning powerful, perhaps life-changing, as you begin to read and reflect on *Lead with Endurance...26.2 Milestones for Improving Life and Leadership!* My challenge to you is to pace yourself at just the right speed, so you too will be another leader who has endured *LwE* and finished your race!

Like any goal or training for running a marathon, the importance of "breaking down" the goal is essential. Rather than diving right into all *26.2 Milestones for Improving Life and Leadership,* I encourage you to think of a race (read and learn) plan. What will be your pace? Who will be your training partners? How many milestones will you cover each day, each week, or each month? How long do you anticipate it will take for you to get to the finish line of this book?

When I train for a particular race, I use a training log to record details such as my training for the day, nutrition, feelings, thoughts, and even confirmation of reaching certain milestones. During your journey of using *LwE* as a tool, it is my hope that you don't rush through without enjoying the process of reading, reflecting, note recording, and taking action on one milestone at a time. May you and your training partners, if you choose, enjoy the training. Hopefully, at times, you too will feel some discomfort, pain, and suffering as your thoughts on life and leadership are challenged along your journey. My fear is that your pace is too quick, which will result in "injury" or worse yet, a did not finish, known as DNF. I will be on the course, cheering for your success, so please get into a rhythm and pace that best fits your training and learning goals. Take the time to read each milestone by building in time to use the "training log" to reflect and take action, recording your thoughts and processing your learning. While reading from cover to cover may provide learning, you will not fully benefit from each milestone unless you find the right pace...it will be your reflection, action, and application that will bring value and relevance. If the pace is too fast, no worries, each milestone will be ready for you to accomplish when you're ready to endure the learning! I am confident, that after finishing this race, you too, will be much better prepared to live and lead with endurance.

May the wind blow at your back as you begin your marathon of learning, growing, and leading. On your mark ... Get Set ... Endure!

Milestone 1 - Purpose

When your purpose is stronger than the challenges you will face, you will endure without surrender, while most others will fold! What is your purpose? Why do you do what you do? To endure the demands of leadership, not only does your organization need to clarify its purpose, but as an individual leader, it is critical that you define your purpose with utmost clarity. Purpose provides drive-strength and passion as it fuels intrinsic motivation to do the work. Purpose energizes and it becomes a means to fulfilling a vision and a mission. A well-defined purpose incites organizations, businesses, teams, and individuals to achieve results! I never clearly defined my purpose as an educator and leader until my second year as an administrator. I attended a national conference in Steamboat Springs, CO as a fledgling assistant principal, and it was during this week-long training institute that I clearly defined my purpose as an educational leader:

- To lead in a way that positively impacts those I serve, both personally and professionally, by providing high standards, feedback, growth, accountability, coaching, and relational connectedness.
- To build systems of support, so those I lead can perform their responsibilities with high performance, which will positively impact teaching and learning by focusing on the essentials.
- To improve people and the organization...to be the highest performing in what we do in the county, state, and why not the nation?

As a 28-year-old, second-year assistant principal, it was on a pre-dawn run in Steamboat Springs, CO, before the morning conference session, where I solidified my purpose as a leader in education. Almost twenty years later, my purpose has only changed minimally.

A well-defined purpose is a beacon that charts the course and allows one to effectively navigate through the tumultuous seas of leadership. In order to have credibility with those you lead, you must first be able to clearly articulate your plan and principles by word and action with compassion and love for those you lead. Confirming your purpose defines your contribution to the greater cause; without it, passion will become stagnant and decisions in the best interest of those you serve will falter. Without a doubt, purpose drives motivation, leading with the intent to help actuate growth.

All of the high performing employees I evaluated and supervised over the years had something in common; high will and/or high skill. As a leader, you can grow employees' skill sets and provide corrective feedback loops to improve performance, but if an employee does not have the will, it's simply time to shift from getting them to grow to getting them to go. People without a purpose become distracted and lose focus. I am convinced that when your purpose is clearly defined, you will have drive-strength to endure the challenges of your role. I remember assisting a young special education teacher early in my administrative career with a difficult, challenging student. It was clear that due to adverse childhood experiences, this particular student had become emotionally impaired. In my experiences, kids become environmentally impaired, often due to an unfortunate upbringing that impacts the mental well-being of the child during the socialization process. On a Friday afternoon, the final day before Christmas break, minutes before the dismissal bell, I was requested to report to the (EI) classroom. In a panic, the teacher explained to me that his student had shimmied his way above the drop ceiling and was "crawling" along pipes to hide from being held accountable for an inappropriate gesture he had made toward another student.

Situations like these are unique and require instinct. However, instinct without a defined purpose could lead to failure. Because my purpose had been clearly defined to lead in a way so those I lead can perform their responsibilities with high performance, which will positively impact teaching and learning, I chose to provide a learning lesson for both the student and this relatively new teacher. Despite the bell ringing for dismissal, and the majority of our 750 seventh and eighth grade students departing the building, eager to begin a two-week vacation from school, I decided to shut the classroom door, and pretend as if we were leaving the classroom, whispering to the teacher to go outside the building to guard the window, just in case the student decided to crawl outside. I remained in the hallway outside the classroom. The "cat and mouse" game began. Thankfully, it was no longer than 10 minutes, the classroom door opened, and I was there to greet our ceiling climber. As this particular student opened the door, once realizing I was waiting, he shouted, "What the fuck are you doing here?" I simply responded, "You can either talk with me or the police, but talking that way with either one will not help you, so which one would you prefer?" I then followed up by saying, "If you choose to speak with me, at least we can grab some dinner on the way home."

Processing the disciplinary action of this student was important, not only for the student but also for the teacher. Without my purpose to help guide me, I am quite sure that I would've lost my temper, overreacted, and not addressed the situation while thinking of how I could not only assist the student but also provide a learning opportunity to help improve the teacher's performance. When leaders empower those they serve, we cause learning and growth opportunities, ultimately improving performance. In the end, this particular student did not want a Christmas break. His actions were the result of him having severe anxiety about not being able to come to school for two weeks. He was afraid of leaving his safety net, an environment that was stable, caring, and took care of his needs. What a powerful learning opportunity for a young teacher and even me to experience. The impact an educator makes on students is powerful!

Making an impact is what leaders do. Leaders with a well-defined purpose are the ones that influence with passion and a deep vow of relentless perseverance to endure challenges because of their purpose. In 1998, I read an article that solidified how a defined purpose can be life-changing as a leader. At the time, I was teaching middle school social studies and coaching varsity cross country. I wanted to find a connection for my students and athletes that would provide inspiration to think about their lives and future with purpose in mind. The article was about a ten-year-old boy named Rudy Garcia-Tolson. The article caught my attention because Rudy was an endurance athlete and he was in preparation to complete his first triathlon. What inspired me is how Rudy did so as a double leg amputee! Rudy was born with popliteal pterygium syndrome, causing several rare birth defects. By the age of five, Rudy had already endured 15 complicated surgeries in an attempt to straighten out his legs. Faced with a lifetime in a wheelchair, Rudy made the decision at that young age to amputate both of his legs. Can you imagine? At the age most kids are learning their ABC's and playing with their friends in a sandbox, Rudy was learning that he would never walk again with his own legs. Over time, through countless struggles, Rudy defined his purpose in life to be a role model for future generations so they don't have to feel held back by any limitations that are placed on them. Rudy's purpose propelled him to win several medals in the Paralympics, and in 2009, Rudy became the first double above-knee amputee to complete a full Ironman Triathlon by finishing the Ironman Arizona. Because of Rudy's purpose, he not only swam 2.4 miles, biked 112 miles, and ran a full marathon of 26.2 miles at the Ironman, but he did so with prosthetic legs, fueled by his purpose, and inspiring future generations that there are no limits. Rudy is a leader in changing the world. Rudy leads with endurance!

Note: The Reflection and Action Workbook section is for you to process and personalize the milestones in whatever manner suits you best. Talk about the questions with a trusted colleague, ponder them while exercising, jot down notes, etc.

Milestone 1 - Reflection & Action: Purpose

1. How does the running leg symbolize health, fitness, and well-being?

2. Do you have a defined purpose for your own personal life?

3. Do you have a defined purpose for your own professional life?

- If yes, let's confirm by writing it out:

Personal

Professional

- If no, take a few minutes to brainstorm your purpose:

Personal

Professional

4. What are the actions you have taken or will take this week that demonstrates your commitment to your purpose?

5. How will defining and confirming your purpose help you endure professional and/or personal struggles?

Milestone 2 - Health, Fitness, & Well-Being

Do you take your health for granted? I am the biggest whiner when I get sick! My wife will attest to my pathetic sniveling and whimpering when coming down with an illness. I would rather run mile repeats in a downpour at dawn than fight the common cold.

Good health is not simply being free from physical ailments; it's having a positive, healthy mindset and a spirit of endurance. For leaders, personal well-being and health are overlooked far too often, as we relentlessly care for others day in and day out. Many leaders have parental responsibilities or the demands of caring for aging or dying parents, resulting in the sacrifice of personal wellness. Ignoring your own health, fitness, and well-being is a reckless course that will eventually cause lifelong implications if not addressed or balanced. To take care of the demands of work and home, leaders must give themselves permission to enjoy the satisfaction of heart-pounding workouts, the pleasure of nurturing friendships, and the peace found in reading, reflecting, and decompressing from the high pressures of life and work. I will staunchly defend those who make their personal physical and mental health a valued priority. While I have often felt guilty for the time and energy I invest in taking care of myself, I have learned that my family and work flourish when I do. It is not selfish to balance your life and take care of yourself. Neglecting your mind, body, and spirit will have devastating consequences on your personal and professional relationships and on your performance and productivity.

It is a mistake to think of ourselves as possessing a finite amount of energy, which exercise only depletes. On the contrary, I believe the human body is like a rechargeable battery that can be perpetually refreshed. In a rechargeable battery, the negative-to-positive electron flow that occurs during discharge is reversed and the battery charge is restored. Just like during exercise...our blood flow is enhanced, which increases the flow of oxygen and nutrients to our muscle tissue and improves our ability to produce more energy. Ironically, exercise actually produces more energy!

During the workday, have you ever found yourself becoming short with others, irritated, and quite frankly, ineffective due to the grind, stress, and pressure of making decisions without a healthy habit to alleviate the pressure? For me, running has been my release, my therapy. During the past several years, I have committed to 90 days of P90X3 to get through each winter. If I go more than three or four days without exercising, my leadership and impact at work and at home suffer. Not only does exercise provide an opportunity to decompress, move oxygen, improve blood flow, exercise is also an escape from technology, email, texting, and phone calls. Years ago, I kicked the habit of bringing my cell phone with me while I exercised because protecting this time away from the demands of work is essential.

The demands of work require healthy eating, hydration, and mental well-being. No one can fulfill this need for you. You must schedule the time and make the commitment, though there will be countless distractions and demands that threaten this vital self-pledge. Based on firsthand experiences, I know that focusing on diet, hydration, and exercise will make a significant difference in the output of work, energy, and performance. Our loved ones will benefit from our health, and we will be giving them our best selves!

During my first year as an assistant superintendent, I presented a 90-day health, fitness, and well-being challenge to our district administrative team of 17 administrators. We focused our efforts around a fun challenge to help us get through the winter months, catapulting our quest all the way to spring break. We calculated daily points based on the following:

Exercise	Rest	Hydration	Nutrition	Texting
30 minutes	8 hours	64 ounces	5 servings	0 - Zero
Must cause beads of sweat. Only category, multiple points are attainable.	May include 7 hours of sleep with an hour of reading, relaxing, etc...	Minimum of 64 ounces of water, trying to reduce and/or eliminate soda	Fresh fruits and/or veggies	No texting while driving
Every 30 minutes = 1 point	1 point	1 point	1 point	1 point

While thrilling to compete and witness the positive impact on my colleagues personally, it was amazing to hear the stories of how families were impacted. Spouses began to change habits. One fellow administrator literally transformed his blood work results within one year due to his focus on health, fitness, and well-being. As a former collegiate wrestler, this particular leader knew how to endure. However, with a consuming job as a building principal, a father of two young daughters, and a busy wife with her own career, he had a wake-up call with a routine annual physical. With high blood pressure and cholesterol, he was sick, despite his physical appearance of "looking" very healthy. He committed to exercising, including cardio and strength training, reduced his intake of salt and sugar, drank water rather than soda, and participated in sessions of yoga for one year. By making health, fitness, and well-being choices a priority, he amazed not only his family and school team, but astounded and inspired his physician because of the overwhelming data. His blood work over one year was completely transformed and healthy without taking any prescribed medications.

To be a leader, we must overcome the notion of being egocentric and vain by taking care of our health, fitness, and well-being. Our loved ones and those we serve are counting on us! Our performance on the job requires us to not only be strong models and great examples but to advocate for and support those we lead. We simply must inspire and encourage self-care. If we don't do this for ourselves, no one else will! As leaders, we cannot excuse ourselves by blaming our busy schedules and myriad of tasks. Whenever I have thought I was too busy to exercise because of the hours or stress of the job, I think of our Presidents who exercised. Many U.S. presidents have found time to exercise regularly while they ran the country, how can we make the excuse of being too busy? Find something you enjoy doing, but get moving. The sixth

U.S. president, John Quincy Adams, was a walker. He walked 2-6 miles every morning. He also had a fondness of swimming nude in the Potomac River in Washington DC. I'm certainly not proposing you go for a skinny-dip in a public location, but at the age of 55, John Quincy Adams challenged himself and made time to exercise to see how long he could swim before touching the bottom of the river. He built his endurance from 20 to 50 minutes. Ronald Reagan was also a fitness leader. Perhaps his career in acting made him realize the benefits of maintaining physical fitness. In 1983, President Reagan wrote an article titled "How to Stay Fit: The President's Personal Exercise Program". Ronald Reagan understood the importance of alternating cardio, strength training, and flexibility exercises into a regular program. President Bill Clinton understood the importance of counting on others for motivation. His choice of exercise was jogging with his secret service squad three or more times each week during his eight years as the president. Finally, George W. Bush and Barack Obama were also fitness gurus. While President Bush trained and ran marathons, President Obama took exercise to a new level. During his presidency, Obama had one of the most stressful jobs in the world, yet he made time to work out on a daily basis. His doctors said that he was healthier than many men half his age. It's a matter of priority. I don't know about you, but these presidents making time for their health, fitness, and well-being is impressive to me.

It should not take a visit to your physician or blood work to tell you that there are many things you can control that will help you at work and at home.

Please consider the following:

- Rest - Get more sleep (7-9 hours each night is considered healthy).

- Physical activity - Find time to exercise: recharge for 30 minutes five times a week.
- Learning - Continue to learn and grow; make time for reading or listening to podcasts.
- Hydration - Drink the right amount of water, based on your current body weight. It is recommended to drink half of your body weight (in ounces). If you weigh 180 pounds, you should drink 90 ounces of water each day.
- Reduce sugar, salt, and processed foods.
- Take deep breaths throughout the day: pause, inhale through nostrils, exhale through the mouth. Concentrate on deep breaths—try 7-8 breaths and see how you feel. Go ahead, close your eyes and try it right now!
- Stay organized by trashing the clutter to reduce stress.
- Complete and encourage random acts of kindness (you'll be surprised how this can help your mental well-being).
- Don't spend time responding to negativity; move forward with your action plan.
- Spend quality time with family. Be present and engaged when with family.
- Find humor in your work, with your friends and family, and in yourself.

Milestone 2 - Reflection & Action: Health, Fitness, & Well-Being

Self- Assessment:

Take this quick, five-question assessment, and be honest and real. This assessment is not intended to compare your results with others unless you feel comfortable to do so. The purpose is to assess your current status.

1. How much sleep per night have you averaged the past week?

2. Do you drink water throughout the day? Yes or No. If yes, how many ounces?

3. How many minutes have you exercised in the past 7 days?

4. Are you eating healthy? Yes or No. Explain your answer.

5. How is your mental well-being? Using a scale from 1 -10,
   1 = Unsafe, 5 = Good, 10 = Great
   Rank: _____ Explain:

Reflection:

Review your self-assessment results and reflect on what you learn. Respond to the questions below:

1. How does the battery symbolize health, fitness, and well-being?

2. How do you feel after exercise and what impact does it have on your day?

3. Identify what roadblocks might inhibit your commitment to personal wellness?

4. How can you overcome or solve these inhibitors so that health and wellness can be your priority?

5. Who will help you improve your health and fitness? List a name or a group that you can count on for accountability.

6. What type of challenge might be proposed to hold yourself and/or a group/partner accountable to take the next steps or improve health, fitness, and well-being? Explain.

Milestone 3 - Circle of Influence

I am grateful for so many people who have influenced my life. Educators have been some of my greatest influencers, along with family members, friends, and professional networks. When I was involved with leadership positions that directly involved students, I would often tell students and athletes, "Surround yourself with positive people and positive things will happen." I recall surprising several parents when I would tell them what type of child they had by making a judgment call based on who their child sat with in the cafeteria, who they interacted with on social media, and the friends they associated with on the weekends. Facing the brutal facts of who we spend time with on a daily basis, shapes our decisions, actions, behaviors, core values, and leadership. Some relationships are distractors that inhibit us from achieving our full potential as leaders. Our best relationships are the steadfast ones that we sharpen ourselves against. It is in identifying our circle of influence, our mentors and empowering people who shape our lives, that we recognize who we have become and who we aspire to be.

While my personal circle of influence has changed over time, I have had some powerful influences for over 47 years. As a leader, our roles and scope of responsibilities are too demanding to do alone. Leaders cannot endure without a support system of faith, family, and friends. Leaders must have people in their circle that can be trusted, unbiased, and unconditionally supportive.

When contemplating a decision that presents a challenge, who do you connect with to seek advice, input, and feedback? Who can you count on to share unbiased feedback when facing personal or professional struggles? Many of the people I have been blessed to have included in my circle of influence have assisted me from personal challenges of raising three boys to professional struggles such as facing formal complaints of bullying and harassing by an underperforming employee. From choosing a family vacation destination to pursuing an $80+ million bond proposal for a school community of nearly 4,000 students and 500 employees, I have relied on the most influential people in my life to provide me feedback, wisdom, and clarity. People within your circle of influence become part of your life and career adventure. Ultimately, they inform your future.

Circles of influence are necessary for leaders, and most gratifying, if you lead well, you will be included in other leaders' circle of influence. Most of the time, being a part of someone's circle is not formalized. There is no contract, agreement, or certificate. Based on relational trust and a vested interest to help grow someone, the circle of influence is established naturally without formalization. However, as leaders, depending on the role and responsibility, it's necessary to add formality to your circle by seeking professional coaches or consultants through contracted services.

Sometimes your circle of influence is circumstantial and short-lived. When I was seeking the best possible treatment plan for my brain tumor, I had a team of medical professionals, multiple doctors from a variety of specialists, all who became part of my circle of influence during an intense, grave period of time for me. Some of these physicians remain in my circle as we continue to monitor my progress. One of these physicians, Dr. Chad Uptigrove, has not only become a great friend but someone I believe will be in my circle of influence for the rest of my life, both personally and professionally. On the flip side, I am honored to be within Chad's circle of influence. While our careers and family structures are very different, we have a bond that brings us together because of our trust, unbiased filtering, and unconditional support for one another.

Regardless of the scope of work we do as leaders, we cannot do it alone. Whether you're a single parent balancing a demanding career and getting kids to and from dance classes or soccer practice or a CEO striking up a multi-million dollar contract overseas, we need others to be a part of the journey. From leading a church, coaching a little league baseball team, or leading a business of 5 or 500, we cannot do this work unaided. To endure, we must have our circles defined!

Milestone 3 - Reflection & Action: Circle of Influence

1. How does this image symbolize the circle of influence?

2. Who has influenced your life and your leadership? Briefly record why each person has influenced you as well. Take the time to fill out your current circle of influence:

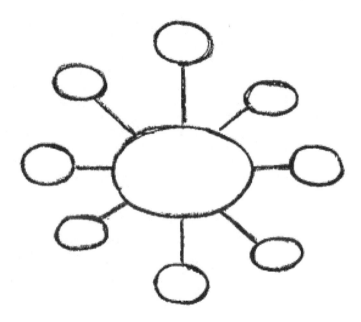

3. Write or send communication of gratitude to each person in your circle of influence. Do not even go onto the next milestone until this task is completed. You have not reached this point in your life without them, so take the time to share your thankfulness.

Milestone 4 - The Voice Within (Intuition)

"So, how did you two meet?" A typical question for a married couple, right? My wife and I don't have a typical response. When I was coaching high school cross country, one of my athletes remained persistent to the point of annoyance about his cousin, Carrie, whom he wanted me to date. Continuously, I gave my canned response, "No worries, Stevie, Coach will take care of his dating life; you just focus on running!" Closing our fall season, we had a beloved team tradition to gather for a Christmas party. Stevie's family was hosting and he had made special arrangements for Carrie to be at his house picking up his little sister for a bowling night at the time I would arrive. As I turned the corner into the kitchen, our eyes locked. Because we were both teaching and coaching at that time, we hit it off right away, and of course, we had a lot of "Stevie stories" to share. I must admit, I neglected my entire team for 30 minutes, and they all knew why!

My athletes and the parents that were at Stevie's house all knew I had a sparkle in my eyes. Following the gathering, I headed to my parents. At the dining room table, my parents were with my aunt and uncle. They asked how the cross country party was and I immediately pronounced, "I just met my wife." Remarkably that night, Carrie met up with her parents who were also with an aunt and uncle, and she claimed that she had just met her husband.

We both knew. The undeniable voice within spoke with resounding clarity. Shortly after, I summoned the courage to call Carrie and our story began. Meeting this incredible match for life, she emanated sincere warmth and kindness, yet I would soon learn her sharp intellect would challenge and keep me on my toes for the rest of my life! Not only did her dark brown eyes seem to dance in the sunlight, but she radiated energy that quickly filled my heart. Little did I know how she would become my greatest source of strength and comfort, building my endurance and pushing me personally and professionally. Crazy in love and fully committed, we were married that very next summer! Twenty-one years and three children later, we are wholeheartedly thankful for Stevie and the voice within that spoke to him so definitely and so persistently.

For me, I often hear the voice within after spending considerable time processing a decision. The voice within is triggered by our subconscious minds, bringing learning experiences of the past to the surface, providing valuable intuition for sound decision-making. Spending years being involved with the hiring process of hundreds of educators in a variety of positions, my intuition has frequently guided me to hiring the best candidates. I don't have hard data to support my claim, but I am confident that the voice within has guided me to the right candidate well before the processing of interviews with the greater committee began. Between 2012 - 2016, I was privileged to hire about 13 administrators while developing a succession plan to the superintendency. At the time, we used a three-round interview process involving multiple stakeholders in the process. We were developing our prized team and aimed to recruit the best and brightest, evaluating our hires with the highest scrutiny. In every case, I relied on the voice within, to drive my final decision. Listening to the stakeholders involved during the interview process, synthesizing formal and informal data, the voice within validated my intuition.

Some people rely on prayer, meditation, or a quiet time of reflection to stir up the voice within; while others rely on the voice within that appears in the moment of battle and offers immediate feedback to help them move forward. Leaders are faced with a flood of decisions each day, often requiring quick immediate responses. The voice within is often an echo of our past experiences, background knowledge, lessons learned, and mistakes made that provide a voice to give us direction. When listening to the voice within, great leaders do what's right, avoiding the temptation of the voice that might say do what is easy.

As leaders, we need to listen to the voice within when we have suspicious thoughts even about people we genuinely care for and with whom we have an established relationship. Dismissing employees can be gut-wrenching, and I was unfortunately accountable for not only dismissing but pressing criminal charges against one long-time employee.

I was the superintendent at the time, and our middle school principal scheduled a meeting with me to discuss a concern. The office team had noticed a discrepancy when conducting a student medication count. They monitored the situation, and a few weeks later, they were confident that someone was stealing the medication. After further investigation, we continued to monitor surveillance and security cameras. On the day we discovered the culprit, my heart sank. While we knew someone was stealing, we were hoping it was not who we thought, simply because of the tight-knit relationship a principal fosters with his or her secretary. Trust is vital, but actions speak for themselves. On a monitor, we clearly saw this particular secretary use a key to enter the medication cabinet, take prescribed medication from students' bottles, and then substitute the stolen meds with a replacement. Authorities believe Ritalin was stolen and replaced with another unknown type of pill. Numb and sick to our stomachs, I remember meeting with our middle school principal to confirm. Horrified, we knew we had witnessed a reckless criminal act and were dreading the severe ramifications that would come down on our secretary and her family. We were also wildly outraged because of the harmful jeopardy she had placed upon our students! We met with the police and arranged for her to be arrested the next morning as she reported to work. Our middle school principal did everything right, and I was proud of the way he protected her dignity, despite such a painful experience to endure. Larceny in a building and obtaining a controlled substance by fraud was the charge she faced. She was facing two felonies, which are punishable by a maximum of four years in state prison. As leaders, the middle school principal and I faced how to communicate and address the fallout.

Despite working with this particular person for over seven years, a very high-performing and popular middle school secretary, the voice within hinted that she may be guilty, but the relational connection would pose doubts. She had three kids, all very active and involved with a variety of sports, and she was also a coach on our staff. Additionally, her husband was a volunteer in our district and was also very well connected to the school community. Escorting her out to the police cruiser and witnessing her arrest was heart-wrenching; it was abundantly clear she was struggling with many significant issues and her family would also pay the price.

Following her arrest, I alerted our staff, parents, and the school community. An excerpt from my letter read:

"While working closely with the Norton Shores Police Department, we discovered clear evidence that misconduct regarding medication counts/inventory occurred. This discovery is particularly disturbing because of the long-term relationships and personal connections this employee has with many of us in our school community. This type of misconduct threatens the safe and secure learning environment at Mona Shores Public Schools and will not be tolerated."

The letter went on to say that the school was cooperating with the Norton Shores Police Department and that there was an ongoing criminal investigation being handled by police. I also asked that community members be sensitive to the family and individuals affected by the situation and to refrain from speculation; especially on social media platforms like Facebook and Twitter.

Sometimes our intuition forces us to make split-second decisions. When I was 12 years old, a quick burst of intuition sparked my voice within and prevented what might have been a much more severe accident that occurred while riding snowmobiles on my aunt and uncle's farm. It was a cold night, and the snow on the ground was fresh and powdery. We were zipping across fields and cow pastures at 80 - 100 mph through near whiteout conditions. I was following my cousin, who had my sister on the back of his snowmobile. Foolishly, we were simply guessing our whereabouts because of the reduced visibility brought on by the heavy windblown snow. At times, I could not even see the taillight in front of me. As with running, I like to lead, and on this night, I was falling behind because I didn't have a clear vision.

Losing sight of my cousin and sister, I pressed the throttle and was building speed to catch up, recklessly flying across an unknown field. I thought it was time to take the lead and senselessly raced by my cousin and sister. Just as I angled across the tracks of their snowmobile, I watched them crash into something. Because of the poor visibility, I didn't know what happened, but I knew both of them had been flung off the snowmobile and parts of the sled had flown up into the air. To this day, I remember the sick feeling of thinking they had just had a fatal accident, crashing into a barbed wire fence used for the cattle herd. The voice within told me to jump. Instantly, my intuition took over and I hurled myself off, narrowly missing my own collision with the barbed wire fence. Desperately searching for my cousin and sister, I ran towards their snowmobile following the fresh tracks from my sled. It was near blizzard conditions as the wind had picked up. My sister's shrieking rose above the howling wind, and I sprinted forth. My cousin was certainly shaken by the crash, but despite the swelling bruises and a cracked snowmobile windshield and hood, they were fortunate. Middle school boys aren't always cautious enough. Had I not jumped off my snowmobile, I could have been killed as I increased speed to take the lead. The voice within recognized danger and saved my life. Sometimes as leaders, we can push too fast, causing others to crash, rush, or make mistakes.

Our ability to endure the fast pace of life and leadership provides us with more experiences to help strengthen the voice within. Experience informs our future. Consider the benefits of listening to the sage voice of a grandmother or grandfather.

Milestone 4 – Reflection & Action: The Voice Within (Intuition)

1. How does barbed wire symbolize the voice within?

2. What does listening to the "voice within" mean to you?

3. How is your "voice within" influenced?

4. Share a time when your intuition, the "voice within", led to an important decision. Explain the situation and outcomes.

5. In your life or in your leadership, where do you need to listen more closely to the voice within?

Milestone 5 - Organizational Culture

Culture will trump a leader's ability to make change. Culture is what drives any organization. Culture is not static; it bounces along like Tigger, abundantly capturing positive energy, or if not careful, the culture may be suffocated with negativity and doubt like Eeyore. If any leader wants to make changes, the culture must be positioned to not only accept change but to sustain change. Too often, leaders fail because they truly believe that because they stated an expectation, gave a directive, or overhauled a system, the new change would be implemented and followed with fidelity. Mistakenly, businesses and organizations place too much emphasis on systems without growing the culture. Regardless of a mission, vision, or purpose, the highest performing teams and organizations are the ones that focus on culture. Culture is all about the people we serve each day and how they live and work together.

As leaders, we must focus on relationships and develop stakeholders to influence the culture of the organization. It is our highest duty to encourage, inspire, and challenge those we lead; we must keep the "Tiggers" bouncing along!

If we are lax and permissive leaders, allowing toxic individuals to damage and undermine our organization, our credibility and respect will be lost. If we ignore toxicity, we condone it, and that is the exact message we are sending to the organization. Removing toxicity, or at least reducing it to a level that does not impede the team's mission and vision, may even require inciting employees to move on if indeed they are unable to grow and change after targeted attempts.

At Orchard View High School, I remember how the culture of one of my varsity cross country teams was challenged when one of our All-State caliber athletes became injured. It was 1998, a week before the City Championships, and one of my future all-state cross country runners twisted his ankle playing basketball before practice. I could not believe one of my athletes could make such a short-sighted blunder, after all, I had told them in no uncertain terms just days before the "Big Meets" began to be cautious, including what I thought was a clear directive to not play basketball! We had made it...we were in the championship season and heading into the City, Conference, Regionals, and the State Championship races. We were not only hungry, but we were healthy as a team. Of course, this particular athlete, A.J. Tumele, knew for himself the mistake he had made. I had coached A.J. since middle school and he had trained hard enough to not only be a frontrunner at each of the championship meets, but we also knew he was fit enough to be an All-State runner. As A.J. hobbled to me before practice, I could see in his eyes that he was bothered. Instantly the tears began to flow, and I remember him saying, "I guess the 500 miles I ran this summer just went to waste." I quickly assured him that if it wasn't broken and because of his 500 miles, we had enough time to get him prepared for the State Championships. It was my intuition!

Getting A.J. to the state meet not only happened, but he ran the second-fastest 5k in school history, running 15:47 and was an All-State cross country runner with opportunities to run in college. How did A.J. go from a swollen, black and blue ankle that wouldn't fit in a shoe, to lacing up his racing spikes and running a lifetime best three weeks later? It was because of our team's culture. A.J.'s teammates cheered him on when he ran in the pool, worked out on the stationary bike, iced, stretched, and kept his mind on the end goal. The culture of our team overcame adversity. While A.J. did not race in the City Championships, A.J. was the biggest cheerleader for his teammates, lifting their spirits to another team title of city champs, despite not having one of our best runners in the state competition, due to his unexpected injury. A.J.'s teammate, Steve Sheffer, was crowned City Champ, and A.J. was his biggest cheerleader that day, instead of running as his competitor. Although A.J. did not help our team with his racing efforts that day, his impact, attitude, and leadership within the team's culture allowed us to win another City Championship title. Enduring obstacles and setbacks are successfully done when the culture of any team is positive!

Culture is a significant factor ... not only for employee retention but also for prospective employees. During the summer of 2009, I struggled with a major decision that ultimately came down to a tug-of-war between two different organizations. Culture drove my decision to leave an elementary principalship that had a phenomenal culture in a school district with tremendous culture, to a building in a neighboring district that was known as the "armpit of the district." I was contacted during the original posting about applying for the position, and after meeting with my Superintendent at the time and reflecting on my six years in the current position, I just couldn't depart from such a positive culture. I respected my boss and had learned and grown so much as a leader under his mentoring. I had found tremendous value in our district administrative team and had given six years of my heart and soul to Reeths-Puffer Elementary...I just couldn't walk away from the staff, parents, and students that I loved so much. Loyalty tugged at my heart.

However, the phone calls to apply for the neighboring district position continued. When Mark Platt, a long-time friend, and fellow elementary principal colleague in the same county called me, I finally began to listen. Mark insisted that my skill set, drive, and leadership was exactly what Mona Shores Middle School needed. He particularly heightened my attention when he said the culture was toxic and they needed someone to come in and transform it. It was after that conversation that I contacted my current superintendent and told him I had a change in heart and was going to pursue the position. Some area leaders that knew of the situation called me crazy, but I like to call it the lure of challenge. I left an incredibly positive culture to make an attempt to impact and influence a toxic culture. While leaving Reeths-Puffer in tears because I loved the people I was leaving and was proud of the culture we had developed together, I must admit, Mona Shores Middle School also brought me to tears of a different kind. A few months into the job, I had fears of uncertainty, doubt, and feelings of being overwhelmed with the enormous task of transforming a culture that was far worse than the central office even knew. But after three years of steadfast work, the tears of being overwhelmed at first became tears of joy that were celebrated because of what we all accomplished together. Five years later, I felt incredibly blessed to have worked alongside so many great educators. Together, we had molded the culture into one of the highest performing middle schools in the county, state, and nation. I was only a small piece of the transformation. The staff and faculty only needed a deliberate focus on organizational culture to create this healthy climate.

I wasn't hired until mid-August, so the first letter I sent to our staff came just days before the school year started. Before I even had an opportunity to meet the entire staff, I placed a phrase in the letter: Eeyore vs. Tigger. I started my letter of introduction with a question: Are you an Eeyore or a Tigger? Two weeks later, I placed two stuffed animals on top of digital clocks high up on the wall. Tigger was placed at the front of our meeting room and Eeyore in the back. At the beginning of our very first meeting together, all 65 staff and faculty entered the meeting room, instantly seeing the connection to the letter. The focus was all about a positive, healthy culture. Five years later, Tigger was still watching over us during our meetings. The culture is the attitude of the people.

Milestone 5 - Reflection & Action: Organizational Culture

1. How does Tigger symbolize organizational culture?

2. Explain your organization's current culture. What is the recent history of the culture in the past year or past 2 to 3 years?

3. How do you know if the culture is toxic or healthy? What are artifacts and evidence of a healthy or toxic culture?

4. Who are the "key players" that have the respect and influence of the group to help you develop and/or enhance the current culture? Explain why.

5. What would your ideal healthy culture look like, sound like, and feel like?

6. What are some strategies you can do this week or next month to enhance the current status of the culture?

Milestone 6 - 3LQ

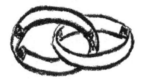

During my time as an elementary principal, I solidified a practice I had used for many years but had never officially termed as a defined leadership strategy. For the sake of formalizing, I named it 3LQ: Listen, Look, Learn, & Question. In my position as a superintendent, I would have 3LQ's scheduled in my calendar with specific visits to each site/building at least twice a month. While it takes time and energy to schedule and implement, I am confident that implementing 3LQ's will provide any leader with valuable data, foster purposeful connections with team members, and also allow for quick accountability checks on systems that have been established. Are expectations, plans, directives, and protocols being followed? How do you know?

Why 3LQ? To tackle the task of making informed decisions, I believe it's best for any leader to become connected with those who do the work. Conducting 3LQ's is simply walking around to connect with people who are on your team, listening to the pulse and buzz of what's happening in the organization amongst team members, looking for evidence of success and opportunities for improvement, and focusing on learning more about individuals, departments, buildings, and finally questioning what you observe to improve the overall health of the organization.

3LQ is a great strategy for a novice leader coming into a new position. It is also a wonderful strategy for veteran leaders as they monitor, supervise, and inspect for quality control and accountability. Most importantly, it is a dynamite strategy for developing, enhancing, and sustaining relationships. 3LQ naturally allows a leader to go beyond just being "visible," but to be fully "engaged" in the mechanics and dynamics of the organization. I avoid attending events simply to be seen and recognized. When attending events, my purpose is to relationally engage with those I serve, using 3LQ to frame my experience into one of tremendous learning; I am not just the boss checking off a visit by standing on the east end of the gym wishing to be noticed.

With any new position of leadership, I have used 3LQ as a launching tool to develop a solid understanding of the current status. Before a leader can actually engage a group of people, he or she must understand the past, gain a perspective on the culture and climate, and seek to understand the current status of all operations within the organization. As a new superintendent, part of my 90 Day Entry Plan consisted of using a 3LQ for my foundation to gain a thorough understanding of the entire district and community. By conducting a three-month 3LQ, representing a "climate survey" with intentionality, I was able to successfully develop a four-year District Strategic Plan that was created by hearing the voices of all stakeholders.

As a new leader in any position, I simply ask members the question,

"Knowing what you know, if you were me, what are three things you would do to make our organization better?" It's amazing how much valuable data is gained. While not necessarily quantifiable, receiving this type of data is profoundly meaningful and relevant because it is based on peoples' experiences, expertise, perspectives, and perceptions.

Listening with a purpose provides incredible data. For years, I posted a sticky note with the following statement on my computer monitor: Ask "What's your opinion?". Many of my decisions were based on synthesizing the opinions of key stakeholders. Listening to your constituents, customers, or employees is the best way to make an informed decision. I have found by simply asking people their opinion on something, a deeper perspective is gained. In addition, seeking input from others provides relevant and authentic data that helps to drive decision making.

As a teacher, coach, manager of a restaurant, or any leadership position, think of the countless ways 3LQ can be used to help you take action after real data is gathered by listening to the voices of the most important people in the organization...the people who do the work. I know in education, many building-level leaders have been trained on how to conduct what are called learning walks, walkthroughs, mini-observations, or learn abouts, but consider how the specific focus and intentionality of 3LQ provides much more in-depth, authentic data for any leader. I have learned that by conducting 3LQ's, the value remains in the interaction and level of engagement that 3LQ provides. There is tremendous value in relationship building, which is the ultimate key for any group/organization/team. 3LQ's take endurance, but like any training, practice, efficiency, and effectiveness are gained. Conducting 3LQ's has been the most impactful and successful strategy I have used in all of my leadership positions.

One of my sons actually conducted a 3LQ at the age of ten without even knowing it. How do I know? My mother-in-love (my preference over mother-in-law) posted the following evidence on a Facebook post in 2015:

I will not put his name on this to protect his identity LOL he is in the fifth grade and it was THAT DAY! Hey you know, the day he had to go to school and learn all about girls!!!! UGH! He came home and talked to his mom about what he had learned. He asked a lot of good questions...."So it's like a race mom, the fastest sperm gets to be the kid, right? Would you have had a different kid if I wouldn't have been fast, or if it would have been a week later, would I not be here today? Can you see the egg?" Mom explained that everything was very small so you can only see it under a microscope. She asked him if he knew what sperm looked like. "Yeah, I know what it looks like, they showed us...it looks like a little fish or tadpole or something. Can we have one as a pet mom?" Poor guy, he is going to have to hear about this when he gets older... lol. Dad is allergic so the guy can't have any pets.....I'm still smiling.....

A great example of 3LQ by a fifth-grade student. Just think of the engagement level if you purposely focus on listening, looking, learning, and questioning, even if it's about "little fish, tadpoles, or something." Someday those "tadpoles" might grow up and plan a wedding.

If you've ever planned a wedding, you probably became an expert at 3LQ. I remember watching my bride-to-be listen, look, learn, and question all of the wedding experts. She didn't miss a detail when talking with reception hall owners, florists, caterers, decorators, musicians, photographers, videographers, pastors, travel agents for our honeymoon, and boutique owners to find the perfect dress for our big day. If you haven't ever been involved with a wedding, let me tell you, they are a lot of work.

As the groom-to-be, I became skillful with the three "L's" ... listening, looking, and learning. One thing I quickly learned was that things would move along much more peacefully if I only engaged in the 3L's and steered clear of the Q's. A bit of advice for grooms out there....don't question too much! A cheerful smile for your bride will go much further than any questioning during this planning phase. A lot of effort goes into planning a successful wedding. A couple must be organized as they begin listening to friends, family members, and authors for ideas; listening to mother nature for the extended weather forecast; looking for locations to hold the wedding and reception; looking for decorating ideas; learning about budgets, costs, and family traditions; learning how to write their wedding vows; and finally, questioning all of the experts to find the best fit for what they're looking for that fits their budget.

Leaders can learn a lot from brides. Most brides are eager to get different perspectives to ensure everything about their special day is extraordinary. As a leader, if you want to impact the culture of the entire organization and create an extraordinary workplace environment, do not overlook hearing the voices of and connecting with your grounds operations crew, custodial and cleaning staff, second or third-party service providers, part-time employees, and other stakeholder groups that have perspective. On numerous occasions, when I was a middle school principal, our daytime custodian, "Mr. Terry," provided me a continuous flow of intel. Terry is exceptionally bright and has the work ethic of a plow horse. A great leader knows that taking the time to listen to others is the best way to grow and make improvements in an organization. If a leader believes their job is to do more talking because it's their job to always have an answer, get ready for a train wreck! By listening to others, a leader gains perspective and follow-ers. By listening to Terry, I gathered data that allowed me to make informed decisions on second shift custodial performances and product purchasing; I was able to identify our mystery smoker (a parent who tossed their cigarette butts out the window in the same location every day in a parking spot identified with evidence); and I learned about his adventures in leadership while he served in the U.S. Army. In turn, I gained a follower and a friend. Mr. Terry made me a better leader! All employees and ranks must be valued and heard to maximize the culture.

Milestone 6 - Reflection & Action: 3LQ

1. How do rings symbolize 3LQ?

2. 3LQ in practice:

New Leadership Role:

As a new leader, how might you use 3LQ to gain a thorough under-standing of the current status of something of interest such as systems, operations, culture/climate, needs, improvement gaps, etc.?

Existing Leadership Role:

As an existing leader, how might you use a 3LQ to check on protocol, procedures, or programs, or processes being followed?

3. Develop a 3LQ series for the next 30 days:

· Who do you need to listen to and why?

· Where will you look (observe) and why? When?

· What do you want to learn and why?

· What questions will you ask and why?

4. After using 3LQ with fidelity, record what you learned. How will you act upon your new knowledge?

Milestone 7 - The Mirror

Some days we recoil at our own reflection, the person in the mirror falling painfully short of who we aspire to be. Rather than assessing our appearance in the mirror, we might use it to reflectively gauge the quality of our thinking, behavior, and leadership. Does the face blinking back reflect dignity and honor? Are we proud of the way we lived and led that day?

Red parachute pants and penny loafer shoes. I finally convinced my parents to enhance my middle school wardrobe with the inimitable style of Michael Jackson, one of my all-time favorite performers. Granted I grew up in the 1980s, but it was MJ who made red parachute pants "cool". Moonwalking to class in penny loafers was the middle school existence. MJ's release of "Thriller" hit the world with a mania that changed the music industry. MJ was a leader because of his work ethic and drive for excellence. MJ was known for perfection, which at times, kept him from sleeping for days because of his passion and pursuit of excellence.

Michael was a competitor, and I could watch him do the moonwalk, dance, and sing for hours and hours. My sister and I would literally argue and fight over the "Thriller" cassette tape we received for Christmas in 1982. Michael endured an endless amount of time in the recording studio and on the stage, fully investing in his rehearsals and going beyond what many artists at the time were willing to do. MJ's song "Man in the Mirror" continues to resonate with me. I believe that when we compete against ourselves, we become better. Jealousy and bitterness come from competing against other people. Look in the mirror...you will find your fiercest competition, and only you know whether or not you fully invested in the work or behaved with integrity.

Thirty years later, the lyrics from MJ's "Man in the Mirror" serve as a great connection to living and leading with honor and dignity.

> I'm starting with the man in the mirror
> I'm asking him to change his ways
> And no message could have been any clearer
> If you wanna make the world a better place
> (If you wanna make the world a better place)
> Take a look at yourself, and then make a change

Now answer me honestly, did you read those lyrics or did you start singing them?

My dad and high school cross country and track coach reminded me to make decisions in a way that I would be able to look at myself in the mirror, knowing I gave the best effort, made the best decision possible, and did the right thing. While all of us must answer or report to people in our lives, whether it's a spouse, boss, coach, or God, we do live with a conscious and subconscious mind. We all know the truth about our own actions. Looking at ourselves in the mirror can be a great daily self-assessment. After all, don't we stand in front of a mirror multiple times a day, at least twice when we brush our teeth? Use this time!

I remember flying out to San Diego, California in 1998 for an invitational elite mile. February 1st of that year was circled on my calendar for almost 9 months as I knew Southern California would be a warm reprieve from the wintry weather of West Michigan. More importantly, I knew the field of milers would be world-class, and I was eager to test myself against the best, competing against 14 runners from around the world and 9 from the United States. The Steve Scott Festival of Races included an elite mile, which was one of the most elite miles in the mid to late 1990s; I was ready to toe the line. Before the race, I looked in the mirror and reminded myself of the hard work and preparation I had given this race. The course was "L-shaped" with a beautiful well-manicured, curbed boulevard down both straightaways. As we assembled for the national anthem and introduction of the 23 athletes, the entire course was lined with spectators stretching a half-mile out. The lead pack was looking to run sub 4:00; my workouts leading up to the race indicated I was prepared to do so.

Striding out the first 400 meters, I was in a perfect place, mid-pack and came through at 59 seconds. Just around the 180-degree turn-around, I was clipped behind and forced to place my hand on the competitors back in front of me, causing two other runners to lose their pace. I quickly refocused, surged, and found myself back in the race. At 800 meters, we had a 90-degree turn, and once again, the pack was tight, and we pushed, elbowed, and jostled for position. I came through on target, running 1:58 and feeling great. We were a pack of about ten runners, all sub 2:00, tightly bunched. At about 1,000 meters, I was forced to the inside along the curb. Just as the pace began to accelerate, the runner next to me caught my arm swing. Faltering for balance, I was tripped from behind, collided with the curb, and stumbled onto the grassy boulevard. Rebounding in a beat, I shot back into the street, but the pack sprinted ahead to glory. Crushed, I let my drive slip away and quit running the race. Returning to the hotel and looking into the mirror was tough. I allowed defeat. Yes, maybe my chances of getting back into the race and running sub 4:00 had slipped away, but running sub 4:05, under those circumstances, would have been acceptable.

The mirror does not lie, and it took months before I completely recovered from knowing I had quit a race. I had "quit" other races, meaning I backed off and didn't give it my all, but to quit a race entirely, this was the first and it has been the last. Enduring means you don't quit. You will stumble and lose ground, but never surrender the race.

Leaders must endure. I remember a special first-grade teacher when I was an elementary principal, who was a fine example of enduring and not quitting on kids. Just before Christmas break, we had a new student enroll. Although we only had a few days before the break, we quickly realized how multiple adverse childhood experiences had impacted this little boy. Verbally and sexually abused by an in-house relative and neglected by lack of supervision and nourishment, this young boy was being raised by his grandmother. Both parents were in prison. Academics were not a priority because his basic needs of shelter, love, belonging, and food had been jeopardized. The behaviors were problematic. During Christmas Break, our first-grade teacher conducted two home visits, spent hours working on a behavior plan, and connected with this child's caseworker to discuss appropriate interventions, support, and strategies. During the winter months, I think our entire lower elementary wing had become exhausted. This young little guy was a spitter, a fighter, and used foul language. I had parents calling me, requesting to have their children moved to another classroom.

Through relentless endurance, refusing to give up on this student, and engaging multiple school and outside agencies, we could look in the mirror with satisfaction for a "job well done". By spring break, not only had his behaviors improved, his reading scores and math scores steadily rose to grade level. At times, I was erring on suspending him from school to simply give staff a break, but the staff refused to let me do so. Why? They refused to quit despite losing focus at times. Each of those educators, while looking exhausted on many occasions, could look in the mirror with pride as they gave their best effort and did the right thing for a student in need.

Milestone 7 - Reflection & Action: The Mirror

1. How does the mirror relate to self-assessing your life and leadership?

2. List a time you looked in the mirror with pride, knowing you endured a very difficult situation. Explain.

3. Identify a time you surrendered your purpose and quit. What would the mirror reflect?

4. How might you use the mirror as a self-assessment strategy to assess your integrity or effort? At the end of the day, what do you want to see reflected in the mirror?

5. Challenge: Go to a mirror (Yes, really try it!) Think of a current project, initiative, or person.

If a project or initiative, ask yourself if you are giving it your very best? How's your work ethic and focus? Explain.

If you thought of a person, ask yourself if you're giving them the attention, guidance, or love they need in order to improve and grow? Explain.

Thinking of your words and actions with family and friends, do they reflect honor and integrity?

Consider your professional words and actions. Do they reflect integrity?

After reflecting, how might you sustain or change your daily life and leadership habits?

Milestone 8 - Go to Gemba

During my elementary principalship, our leadership team attended Lean Training through the Pawley Lean Institute out of Oakland University. Here I learned about "Going to Gemba," and I have been practicing ever since. The term "Gemba" originated as a Japanese word that literally means "the real place" and is used in areas of leadership and management as an improvement strategy. I have used "Going to Gemba" to improve efficiency in lunch lines, playground and recess procedures, classroom management, bond proposals, athletic team warm-up routines, letterhead consistency, flag and flagpole conditions, and even assessing the condition of paint and carpet inside classrooms, along with many other areas that needed improvement.

I recall one of the assistant principals I worked with at Mona Shores Middle School, sitting down with me sharing his concerns about the lunch line. Students were using styrofoam trays and due to the flimsiness of the trays, students were not choosing certain foods for fear of dropping their food. What could we do? I had our food service director and both assistant principals join me in the cafe to go to Gemba. Yes, we waited in line with the students and went through the process as if we were a typical student ready for a hot lunch. I could tell that our food service director was a bit annoyed and thought I was crazy to conduct such an assessment.

What did we learn? It was difficult to hold onto the trays and we desperately needed a serving guide so students could slide their trays down the line, rather than rely on holding their tray. The cashier checkout needed the tubular tray slide removed and a solid surface installed to eliminate this issue. We also noticed that our condiment and plasticware carts needed adjustments to provide efficiency for access. We asked questions while in line, and the students provided us valuable feedback. We then met with the food service staff and benefited from hearing their perspectives.

Following our Gemba visit, we processed our observations and conversations before developing a list of priorities for improvement. To endure as a leader, you must get out of the office and go to the real place and experience a system for an accurate assessment. Only after you've lived it, can you make meaningful and effective change.

Milestone 8 - Reflection & Action: Go to Gemba

1. How does the lunch tray symbolize going to Gemba?

2. Where might you go to look for the current status, seeking ways to improve something within your organization? Explain the location and the concern or problem that could use some improvement:

3. Plan a Gemba:

· Where will you go?

· What will you look for and how will you record your evidence? What will you see, hear, touch, and experience?

· When?
· Who will attend with you, if anyone?

4. What is your goal for conducting this particular Gemba?

5. After your Gemba, reflect, take notes, and develop an action plan for improvement.

Milestone 9 - See Their Eyes

Looking into someone's eyes can be a powerful way of communicating and receiving feedback; however, as a leader, seeing from the eyes of those you lead is a perspective that brings tremendous value. I have failed too many times being incredibly passionate, confident and excited about an idea, initiative, or improvement process because I overlooked the perspective of those the idea would impact. As leaders, we are change agents, and despite seeking change for the common good, we will fail if we don't see our ideas from the eyes of others.

Have you had an inspired stroke of genius, an idea, that you just knew would bring desired shifts and incredible value to your organization? Great leaders are constantly thinking of areas to improve within their organization. While well-intentioned, our productive brainstorming backfires on us! The source of the idea was born in us as leaders, and we have spent days, weeks, and months processing and planning to bring this initiative to fruition. As we begin to roll out the idea, an idea that has only been viewed from our personal lens, it becomes a "flood" or onslaught for those hearing it the first time. Our excitement and passion for the idea, albeit a great idea, becomes shot down due to the overwhelmed feelings of those who are hearing the news for the first time. The failure is not the idea; it's the lack of enduring through a process that allows the leader to see from others' eyes. It is vital to have "buy-in" from those we lead, and how we introduce, frame, and invite our team into the initiative is just as important as the initiative itself. Failure to gain the perspective of others is a failure of developing and influencing change in the most efficient and effective manner; it is compromising to the health of the organization and disrespectful to those we serve.

Leaders who spend time looking from the eyes of others and also care enough to look into the eyes of others to seek input, feedback, and collaboration will ultimately cultivate a culture of shining eyes. We can't bombard those we serve. Slow down, connect, and look into the eyes of those you lead with the mindset that they matter, their perspective is valued, and you care about each team member as a person.

When my youngest son, Landon, was ten years old, I was able to experience a deer hunting season from his eyes. During the fall of 2017, I hunted with Landon eight different times, either sitting in a small double portable treestand about 20 feet off the ground, or in a 5' x 5' hunting shack. On all of our hunts, spending over 25 hours sitting next to each other, we were not only able to enjoy the beautiful outdoors of Michigan, but we were able to talk and connect. Landon is our talker in the family. He is intensely expressive, passionate, and sometimes doesn't know when to stop talking. You will typically hear him before you see him! Because our family hunting property is about two hours away from our home, we also spent a considerable amount of time talking while traveling on several weekends that fall.

The fall of 2017 was one of the most memorable hunting seasons because I was able to experience hunting from the eager eyes of a first-time hunter. While we sat together during our hunts, we were able to whisper throughout just about every hunt, even talking while watching deer less than 20 yards from us. Teaching Landon about how to prepare our equipment for the hunt, the differences between a mature deer and a yearling, looking carefully to never shoot a button buck, discussing the mating season or rut, watching the sun rise and set, and challenging his thinking on the cardinal directions, deer management, wind directions, scent control, taxidermy, taking ethical shots, economic impacts of hunting, and feeding and bedding habits of the deer, it was experiencing the hunting season with new enchantment. The sparkle in his eyes and his constant fury of questions brought tears to my eyes—the joy was too sweet. During his first hunting season, Landon successfully harvested a seven-point buck during the youth hunt, using a 25.06 Browning firearm, and brought home two does for the freezer during the archery season.

Seeing Landon's eyes aglow when he took each of his deer was something I will never forget. Thankfully, I was able to record two of his successful hunts on video. Watching this was a powerful reminder of not only taking the time to slow down in life and be 100% present and fully engaged with my kids, but it also served as a vital experience of seeing something that I knew well from the eyes of someone I led. The 2017 hunting season was my 34th hunting season, yet it was one of the most enjoyable hunting seasons because it was seen through the lens of a youngster experiencing something for the first time. As leaders, to endure the demands and pressures of our roles, we must take the time to slow down, become fully engaged, and appreciate the experiences through the eyes of others. By doing so, we just might find that sparkle that will lead us to a new sense of rejuvenation and enjoyment.

Sometimes, rather than a sparkle in someone's eyes, as leaders, we see guilt. On two occasions, I had to deal with intoxication within the workplace. Both were situations in which I could clearly see the guilt, shame, and embarrassment when questioning the behavior. One was an employee and another a 14-year-old eighth-grade student.

Upon being notified by a colleague about an employee reporting to work late and smelling of alcohol, I asked this particular employee to report to my office. I had another administrator join us in my office. I notified the employee that I was alerted to the fact that she was late to work with the smell of alcohol on her breath, so I needed to ask her some questions. I offered her union representation and assistance as I told her my investigation could lead to discipline. Right away she denied she was under the influence of alcohol. She told me she was not feeling well and fell back to sleep and missed her alarm clock; therefore, she was late. She then mentioned that it was probably her mouthwash that made her breath smell like alcohol. As she explained, continuing to speak without clarity, the smell of alcohol filled the office.

Based on my experience of questioning hundreds of students and adults over the years, I felt she was lying; I could see guilt in her eyes. After pressing for clarification on the difference between mouthwash and alcohol, she shifted in her seat, chin tucked, and the tears began to roll down her face. I could tell by her mannerisms, voice, and behavior that she appeared to be under the influence. We took her to the hospital and she was tested. Her blood-alcohol level at 9:00 a.m. exceeded the levels to drive a vehicle. At the hospital, I expressed my sorrow and ardent desire for her to seek treatment. Unfortunately, I also had to explain that we would be terminating her immediately. We could see the anguish in her eyes as she apologized and explained that she didn't mean to let me down. As I walked out of the hospital, I had tears in my eyes. Enduring difficult situations is tough, especially when you care about the people you lead.

Middle school students are the absolute best! They are filled with wild energy and exuberance, but they can also battle issues of belonging and self-esteem. They demand freedom and test boundaries as they skirt the edge of childhood and young adulthood. During what was supposed to be a fun day at school, where we were recognizing and celebrating student achievement with a field day, cookout, and an afternoon of games and activities, one of our suspended students, decided to show up anyways. I was alerted that we had a student under the influence of alcohol on campus. When I approached the student, our eyes met, and I knew he was a mess. He also knew that my eyes meant business. He bolted, heading toward a group of students. Thinking about the safety of our students and staff that were outside, I took off after him, calling 911 for assistance. Unbelievably, he was so drunk that he stumbled to the ground, and I was able to safely keep him from our student body. Desperate and cornered, he kicked and swung at me, and I struggled to keep him safely restrained until officers arrived.

Meeting with the police, the student, and his mother, I could see the pain in their eyes and knew this family was dealing with some tough issues. Not only was this young teenager drunk, but he was also high, as he admitted to smoking a joint just before coming to school. I could see the frustration in his mother's eyes, and I knew this kid quite well, serving as his assistant principal for two years. As he staggered out the door, he turned around, shook my hand, and told me he would go to counseling and get some therapy. Our eyes connected once again...this time his eyes told me a different story....he was committed to resurrecting his life.

Milestone 9 - Reflection & Action: See Their Eyes

1. How do these eyes symbolize see the eyes of those you lead?

2. Considering your team, what is the difference between looking *into* their eyes and looking *from* their eyes?

3. Share an idea you fostered in your own mind that failed due to a lack of perspective and buy-in from your team.

4. How might you look into the eyes of those you lead to let them know their voices are valued? Who needs you fully engaged and present? Why?

5. As a leader, who can you spend time with or what can you experience that will rejuvenate and reclaim the sparkle in your eyes?

Milestone 10 - The Competition

Every highly effective leader I've known thrives on competition. Healthy and inspiring, competition drives motivation, fuels action, and gives us a purpose to endure the work. When employed properly, I firmly believe competition is something exemplary leaders use to their advantage, persevering through the grind of hard work, challenges, and struggles when most will fold.

One Saturday night, during the junior year of my collegiate indoor track season, a group of guys stopped by our house to recruit more party buddies. Of my six roommates, five of us were on the roster for the upcoming track season. While the promise of great fun was tempting, I was too focused on the upcoming track and field season and qualifying for the NCAA National Championships. Rather than being distracted and giving competitors an advantage, I decided to run 10 miles, because, in my mind, I was outworking the competition. Through the blistering January winds, I resolutely hammered out those miles, outpacing my future competitors in the icy darkness. Desirous of uncommon results against my competitors, I was willing to do the extraordinary.

Grinding through the final third of my distance, I did something deliberately and entirely focused on competition. Despite the snowfall and lack of solid footing on the roads, I clipped off a 6:00 mile pace for the last three miles. Physically, I wanted to puke. I wanted to push through the pain and run the last three miles at a pace that would be tough to endure. In my mind, I thought I would be much better off puking from a training run rather than puking from too much alcohol. I didn't puke at the end of the run, but I do recall laying in a snowbank at the end of our driveway feeling the fire in my legs and lungs. It was nearly 10:00 p.m. and I knew I had just beat the competition. I thought it would be much better to recover from the pain of a training run than sitting around on the couch or in bed on a Sunday morning with a hangover. In my heart, I knew this decision and this night would pay off when I faced the competition three months later.

More important than paying attention to the competition, leaders must challenge themselves and those they serve to compete within themselves. This is the most influential leverage we can find. Finding ways to ignite the intrinsic motivation to "compete" and improve the current status of a particular skill set, project, or goal is our everyday purpose.

Delaying gratification and deliberately enduring hard work leads to optimum results, and this is what "winning" is all about. While winning has multiple definitions when it comes to leadership, my thoughts have been centered around being the highest performing district in the county, state, nation, and why not the world? Paying attention to the competition is important, but it should not change your mission, vision, or values. Focusing on self-improvement and the variables that YOU control is where true gains can be made. Paying attention to the competition should be used to assess whether you're staying ahead of those you compete against. If falling behind the competition, many leaders will think they need to switch and do what the competitor is doing. If so, we only rise to the level of our competitors. The goal should be measured by staying ahead of the competition, which means we have to adjust what we can control and grind-it-out!

One of my favorite stories about competition comes from the Bible, the first book of Samuel. On a battleground separated by a deep valley, the Philistine army was in position for war against Israel. Goliath, a Philistine giant, who was believed to be over eight feet tall and wearing full armor, came out each day for forty days, mocking and challenging the Israelites to fight. Goliath successfully intimidated King Saul and the entire Israelite army. Prepared to endure a battle, David, barely a teenager at the time, was ready to face the competition. Dressed in his simple tunic, carrying his shepherd's staff, sling, and a pouch full of stones, David approached Goliath. Goliath once again tried to use intimidation tactics by cursing at David, shouting threats and insults. As Goliath moved in for the kill, David reached into his bag and slung one of his stones at Goliath's head. Finding a hole in the armor, the stone sank into the giant's forehead, and he fell face down on the ground. David then took Goliath's sword, beheaded and killed him. David faced the competition, he endured the pressure of fear, and his leadership allowed the Israelite army to face the competition of the Philistines. Because of David, the Israelites took over the valley and beat the competition. If it wasn't for a skinny teenage shepherd boy taking on Goliath the Giant, the Israelites' army would have remained docile and fearful of moving forward. Dauntless, David tapped into his inner courage, propelling the defeat of an insurmountable opponent. Competition fuels performance, making us braver and more focused than ever before. Face it, embrace it, and harness the power to realize your organization's greatest gains.

Milestone 10 – Reflection and Action: The Competition

1. How does the slingshot symbolize the competition?

2. Thinking of your work or a defined target goal, who are you competing against?

· List the defined target goal:

· Who are the competitors?

· Are you working on the goal alone or is this with others?

3. What are specific ways you can equip your team to move ahead of the competition?

4. How might competition be used to drive motivation for you and/or your organization?

Milestone 11 - OCF Communication

People forget without repetition. OCF...Old stuff, current stuff, and future stuff is a simple way to ensure repetition of communication. OCF Communication is a strategy I use by realizing how valuable repetition is for understanding. The greatest obstacle between any two in a relationship is miscommunication, and in many cases, miscommunication is due to a lack of repeating until the recipient understands. Just because "You said so" does not work, even when you're the boss. Is what you said understood? Is what you said learned?

Communication is a skill that requires repetition. How often have you emailed a communication and realized that your communication failed because not 100% of your audience responded to your message, request, or directive? Have you ever heard someone say, "I emailed that out, I can't believe they didn't do it?" I have learned that important communication must be done incrementally and repeated often. I have used a format of communication that continues to repeat accounts from the past, provide current topics that are presently on the table, and share a glimpse of the future by sharing hints of what will be coming.

Over the years, I have been asked how long you should continue to revisit communication from the past? My response is simple...until whatever you expected or communicated has been mastered or fulfilled based on your standards. Chunking communication with these three modes of categories can keep important tasks as a focus. At times, it takes a different approach and keeping certain communications in the "old stuff" category allows you to repeat in a different way, or simply provide enough repetition until you have accomplished your original purpose of communication.

Old Stuff - Communication from the past that you deem important, continuously communicating in a variety of modes and in different ways until the purpose is mastered or fulfilled.

Current Stuff - Communication that is in-the-moment, items that need to be known now, hot on the radar.

Future Stuff - Communication that provides a future glimpse of what is to come, which allows others to offer input, feedback, and thinking before the topic becomes a current topic, preventing feelings of being overwhelmed.

Communicating old stuff repeatedly in different ways and in different rates can help ensure understanding. Communicating "current stuff" is best understood when a leader has already introduced the topic in the past and has already planned for future repetitions. Communicating "future stuff" requires leaders to be thinking ahead, knowing what will eventually be "current stuff" on the agenda. Leaders are always thinking ahead. Communicating with a proactive mindset will help your communication stick. Using OCF as a format of thinking, organizing, and communicating has not only enhanced my communication skills in a variety of leadership roles but has also made me a better communicator at home. For parents of children who participate in activities such as music lessons or sports, have you ever found yourself in a panic to find a missing uniform, music book, shin guard, water bottle, or a certain undergarment that is sitting in the washing machine still soaked? Instilling OCF communication increases ownership and responsiveness among the members of a family, team, or organization. It quite simply perpetuates "same-page thinking" and collective action for upholding team commitments. The chart below provides a perspective from each mode of OCF communication that can be applied to any communication for quality results:

Communication	What	When	Home Example	Work Example
Old	Communication previously shared	Repeat until mastered or expectation fulfilled	You might want to check your dresser to see if your white uniform is washed	As a reminder, our new norm is no emailing and texting during our meetings
Current	In the moment	On the spot	Please get dressed with your home colored uniform and be ready to go in 10 minutes	Let's avoid emailing and texting during our meeting today
Future	A future glimpse of what is to come	In advance, sometimes multiple times before making it current	On Saturday, it looks like rain, so don't forget to pack your rain gear, extra socks, gloves, and your water bottle	Beginning next month, to help us focus during our time together, we will look at a strategy to reduce distractions

Milestone 11 - Reflection & Action: Communication, (OCF) Old, Current, and Future

1. How does the circular arrow symbolize (OCF) old, current, and future communication?

2. Where do you spend most of your time in communication? (Old, current, or future)

3. What are the benefits of using all three areas when developing a communication plan?

4. How might your communication be organized with old, current, and future categories to help improve understanding, enhance follow-through, and improve results?

Milestone 12 - Systems Thinking

Systems thinking is a holistic approach that focuses on the way an organization interrelates with flow, function, and efficiency. Rather than departments, cohort groups, or stakeholder groups within the organization functioning in silos and working independently, the systems thinking approach brings alignment and synergy to the full team. Systems thinking is an essential component of a learning organization. Leaders are impacted by technological innovations and global thinking unlike ever before. Systems thinking provides a model of alignment that efficiently assists with decision-making. Adapting to change and improvements for the organization in regards to action steps and strategies can be messy. Systems thinking naturally focuses on collaboration and working together, thinking macro-centrically rather than egocentrically.

Developing systems takes a lot of work, but once accomplished, efficiency, consistency, and productivity will improve your leadership impact. An example of systems thinking takes me back to when I was a Superintendent, driving around the District, conducting a Gemba to look at the condition of our flagpoles and flags. I decided to do a Gemba assessment because I had noticed some differences in the standard, but was unsure how much each site differentiated. Remember, Gemba is a Japanese word that literally means "the real place", used in management as a strategy to go and experience an area in need of improvement.

As superintendent, I wanted alignment in exterior features among the buildings of our district, and I began with the inconsistencies of our flags and flagpoles. I asked our Operations Director the status of our flag poles around the district. He said, "Very good, we check them when we mow." At the time, our District had seven building sites, and in some cases more than one flagpole at a site. I asked about who "we" means when referring to flagpole checks, followed by wondering how he knew whether or not they were checked. After scheduling a Gemba to go look at each flagpole, what did we notice? The observations were disappointing, but it allowed for a great opportunity to begin improving by implementing systems thinking.

After our Gemba, we noticed some flagpoles were in desperate need of repair, including new paint, rope, and even new flags. Flags were also different sizes. Ashamed, we both recognized torn and weathered flags. We also discovered that some flagpoles did not have lights and no one was being held accountable to assess and replace weathered flags. Some flagpoles had 50th-anniversary flags that were over eight years old. Some flagpoles had nautical flags, some did not. Some flagpoles flew the State of Michigan flag below the U.S.A. flag, some did not have our state flag. Creating a system was easy. We developed a plan to agree on a standard for each flagpole and a calendar of when and who would monitor the standard to ensure we had a system in place that met the standard of expectation. Thinking of systems improves the organization by being proactive, developing standards, and providing a protocol of accountability.

Systems thinking is a mindset focused on providing cohesion and congruence among various parts of an organization, building and establishing consistency. This approach will ensure that your customers, students, or whomever you serve will have a common and exemplary experience. In the case of flagpoles, each building site had a different system of standard and monitoring. As an organization, through systems thinking, we not only saved time, money, and resources, we established a standard of expectations that would allow us to fly our American flags with pride.

Milestone 12 - Reflection and Action: Systems Thinking

1. How does the flag symbolize systems thinking?

2. What is systems thinking?

3. Where might you consider developing systems thinking to improve an area you supervise, manage, or lead? Where will you "go" to look for improvements and alignment?

4. Who will assist you with systems thinking and how will you know if you have an area in which systems thinking will bring value?

Milestone 13 - Strengths and Blind Spots

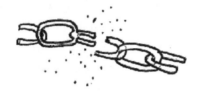

We all have strengths and blind spots, and effective leaders not only enhance their strengths but also learn how to reduce the negative impact of their blind spots. Too often, we take our strengths for granted, and we must not only recognize and celebrate strengths but continue to find ways to grow and build upon these gifts. On the flipside, blind spots can only be addressed if we as leaders humble ourselves enough to receive truly candid feedback from trusted sources. You're everyone's friend until you start telling the truth, so sharing feedback and receiving feedback must be wanted and desired, otherwise, criticism of blind spots will quickly erode any relationship. Establishing trust is a major factor in the role of leadership!

There are multiple assessments and companies that provide personality, management, behavior, and/or leadership traits for individuals or organizations. I strongly encourage you to begin with yourself and analyze the results, which will provide data in regard to your strengths and blind spots. There is no substitute for self-awareness. As leaders, seeing to maximize our influence of others, we must first fully understand ourselves. For over 18 years, I have used (MBS) Management by Strengths as a resource tool to provide this particular analysis.

Teams are capable of performing at higher levels once they know each other's strengths and blind spots. Performance grows exponentially when leadership teams intentionally implement activities and scenarios to apply the understood results. Often, before contacting or meeting with someone within a team, I will quickly review their strengths and blind spots before framing my approach. For example, if I know someone is very direct and prefers a quick chat; their blind spot is an aversion to lengthy discussion and processing of information, I tell them pointedly that I need 30 minutes to discuss a topic and ask when we might connect to do so. Rather than overwhelming them with an unexpected meeting, I provide them the opportunity to decide when is the best time, and I explain that it's going to be a discussion for about 30 minutes. If I went right into a long conversation, I would not have been honoring their preference for being direct.

Using MBS to identify my temperament traits and preferences as a leader, I have learned to combat my blind spots when meeting or speaking with people. In my case, no doubt, my strengths have become my blind spots at times, causing errors and misinterpretations by those I have worked with over the years. The chart below, as an example, explains my strengths and blind spots:

Leadership Trait	Strength	Blindspot	Considerations
Extroversion	People-oriented, like teamwork and working with other people. Talkative and influential.	Thinks aloud through talking and processing, not a good listener.	Be sure to be an active listener and share equitable air time.
Directness	Focus on results, being in control, and problem solver. Get-er-done attitude.	Rushes through on a decision without collaboration. Appears to be intimidating, too confident	Involve stakeholders with decision making and processes. Let others do the work, delegate

Our strengths can certainly become our blind spots. However, once your blind spots are recognized and accepted, it's up to you to act upon considerations and strategies to combat your blind spot for the benefit of those you lead. Recognizing our strengths and our improvement areas is vital to our endurance as leaders. We will find strength in making ourselves vulnerable by listening and living into the valuable feedback from those we love and lead.

Milestone 13 - Reflection and Action: Strengths and Blind Spots

1. How does the chain-link symbolize strengths and blind spots?

2. As a leader, what are your strengths and blind spots? Why? How do you know?

- Do your thoughts align with others that work or live with you?

3. Who can comfortably and candidly help you identify your blind spots without you judging them or it negatively impacting your relationship?

4. When is the last time you have asked a coworker or spouse about your strengths and blind spots? If not within the last year, do so.

- Who will you ask?

- When will you ask?

- Be sure to explain that you want honest, candid feedback

5. What might you do for a group of people you closely work with to seek an analysis report on their leadership preferences/traits? Should you do one first?

Milestone 14 - Positive Strokes

Positive reinforcement is one of the single best strategies to not only mold desired behavior but to also serve as a constant reminder and redirection for less desired behaviors. Catching people doing the right things at the right times is a climate and culture builder because you are individually impacting the organization one individual at a time. Positive strokes can be done in a variety of ways and I have found that providing positive strokes not only shapes desired behavior, but it shifts the organization's focus to a positive, healthy culture. Positive strokes must be authentic by establishing sincerity and trust among those you lead.

Because your goal as a leader is to impact each individual, which in turn, impacts the entire team/organization, be sure to be equitable in your positive strokes. Frequently provide genuine relevant feedback. Establishing a culture of positive strokes will allow you to endure the difficult times, and also provide you relational leveraging when needed.

Showing gratitude is a small task with monumental impact; the returns are endless. Sharing your gratitude, when meaningful, relevant, and specific, leads employees to feel valued, appreciated, and significant. Take time to share your gratitude by providing as many positive strokes as possible. I have never heard a great leader say that they regretted sharing their gratitude and giving positive strokes to people they lead.

Positive Stroke Ideas:

- Call the spouse of an employee or team member and share your gratitude about their husband/wife, while thanking the spouse as well.
- Call a parent of an employee or team member and let them know how proud they must be by sharing an impact their daughter/son is making on the organization.
- Write a handwritten note, expressing appreciation.
- Craft a voice memo and send it via text.
- Interrupt their work in front of others and give them a dose of acknowledgment while in the act of doing what you expect.
- Send a Bitmoji with a positive message.
- Place a piece of candy and a note in their snail mailbox.
- Place a hand on someone's shoulder, look them in the eye, and tell them why you're proud of them and thank them for their efforts. Tell them why they make a difference!

Can you imagine being face-to-face with a 25-foot killer whale? One of my favorite books is by Ken Blanchard, titled, *Whale Done*. This particular "parable" demonstrates successful leadership based on lessons learned by motivating people from an unlikely source. The lead character in *Whale Done* learns from the trainers at the Sea World show in Orlando. Specifically, the discovery is how trainers get the whales to perform certain actions.

Blanchard's fundamental lesson of *Whale Done* is the knowledge and understanding that we can get better results from the people we lead if we provide positive strokes while clearly defining "what is right" and expected. Highlighting, rewarding, or acknowledging desired actions is great reinforcement. The authors point out that the more positive strokes we provide to a desired behavior, the more likely it is that the behavior will be repeated – thus, if we are constantly playing "gotcha" with those we lead who make mistakes, we're actually heightening their attention to the wrong results. Instead, the authors suggest that we constantly encourage employees when they do something right, as a means of giving them the motivation to do it right again in the future.

Indeed, the authors break down potential responses to employee behavior in four ways, based on whether the employee has done something wrong or right. Blanchard explains that "whale done" praise has four steps:

1. Praise people immediately
2. Be specific about what they did right
3. Share your positive feelings about what they did
4. Encourage them to keep up the good work

The ultimate goal of providing positive strokes is to help people become self-motivating, where they associate good feelings with doing their jobs correctly. If the trainers at SeaWorld want a five-ton killer whale to jump out of the water, they must begin with small, incremental steps such as having the whale swim over a rope that is on the floor of the pool. By providing several positive strokes, the rope or "line of height" can be elevated. If the whale does not swim over the rope or does something wrong, redirection is necessary. Blanchard discusses how a redirection strategy is used when an employee makes an error – redirect the attention either back to what they were supposed to do, or to an alternative task. The idea is that you want to focus attention on the task yet to be performed correctly, rather than the mistakes already made. Again, it's focusing on positive strokes. Redirection is accomplished by the following five steps:

1. Describe the error as soon as possible, clearly and without blame.
2. Show the negative impact.
3. If appropriate, take the blame for not making the task clear.
4. Go over the task in detail, making sure it's understood.
5. Re-express your confidence and trust in the person.

The purpose of redirection is to set up a positive response in the future, so that those you lead actually learn, like the whales, to repeat the good behaviors. Negative attention and negative energy will wear on you as a leader! By focusing on the positives, you will be able to lead with endurance and endure the negatives that need redirection.

Milestone 14 - Reflection and Action: Positive Strokes

1. How does the whale symbolize positive strokes?

2. How might you keep track and organize a plan to provide everyone under your leadership with a positive stroke? When will this be accomplished?

3. Choose one of the positive stroke ideas listed above that you would feel comfortable trying:

- When will you try it?
- Who will you provide a positive stroke to?

4. What is the most effective strategy you use when providing positive strokes?

5. How might you develop a pattern of providing positive strokes to those you lead and redirection when necessary?

6. Follow Blanchard's steps to providing a positive stroke. How did your loved one or your employee respond?

Milestone 15 - Eliminate Distractions

Do you focus on what is popular or proven? As a leader, enduring the irritation of one sales marketer reaching out to you one after another is a reality. Someone attends a conference, reads a tweet, or watches a YouTube video, and they come to you with the next best idea. These distractions can drive you crazy! Too often leaders are swayed by promising voices selling them the latest and greatest without ever mastering the current status with fidelity. There are many best practices, but rather than narrowing the focus to become masterful in one area or exceptionally proficient in a few, we recklessly shift to embrace the next popular sales pitch, chasing another program, resource, or the person who has the acclaimed solution. As a leader, don't let distractions sabotage your goals!

Leaders can protect their employees by road-blocking distractions or taking mundane compliance tasks off the plates of the employees who have much more important work to do. Saying "No, thank you" and unsubscribing from the marketing emails that flood your inbox should feel good knowing that you are keeping the focus on what's essential for your mission, vision, core values, and goals. As leaders, we can and should encourage innovation and experimentation, allowing for trials and "pilot" implementation, dismissing or implementing based on results in relation to organizational goals.

Adamantly protect those who do the work from any training fads that threaten to compromise the team vision. Adopting any new initiative, program, or resource for your business requires careful vetting to ensure the product is not only proven but also aligns with your goals. While I'm a champion for change and growth, I do not support change that isn't purposeful or that doesn't directly serve our team's focus and mission. Saying "no" is sometimes the best thing a leader can do for the organization! We need to say "no" more often.

My wife and I have had to say "no" to our three boys often. Kids love to ask, and at times, beg, plead, and bargain for the next popular thing. From wanting drones, fidget spinners, the latest technology craze, or something they saw on social media, or a coveted item a friend has, to wanting a puppy or other pets, we have heard all about what is popular and on our boys' wish lists. During the summer of 2017, our youngest son became obsessed with the popularity of drones, thanks to well-placed ads on his social media. Landon just had to have a drone. Despite our attempts to tell him that it would be a waste of money and that his drone would just be broken in days, he insisted. He used his savings from a lemonade sale to buy a $25.00 drone. He was convinced that his drone would fly for years to come. It lasted about an hour, crashing into the branches of a white pine tree and breaking the propellers. But this was not the first time he would experience frustration. After multiple trips to the store for an exchange, upgrade, and repairs, we exhausted our patience. Eventually, even Landon gave up. Popular versus proven can also be great learning lessons for kids. Similarly, in life and leadership, it takes mistakes to really cement the learning.

When I was superintendent, as a reminder of focusing on what is proven versus what is popular, I wrote the following message on a whiteboard, so our Cabinet (Directors) could clearly see it upon entering for our leadership team meeting:

- Eliminate distractions because you care!
- Eliminate distractions for those we lead because we value their time!
- Eliminate anything not connected to our strategic plan (posted on a whiteboard) because the strategic plan is our focus.
- If it's proven and aligns with our district strategic plan, go for it, otherwise, don't waste my time asking about popular next fads without evidence of proof.

I remember having a great discussion and providing clarity on our focus during this particular meeting. It was amazing how many current and real distractions we discussed during this meeting. We all recognize and acknowledge distractions when we have a focus. Our directors left refreshed knowing they had my permission to ignore the "noise" of marketing distractions and fads that bombard inboxes, voice-mails, and arrive unexpectedly via our networks. I have told many leaders that I have a common response to distractions, including salespeople and marketers: "No thanks" or "Sorry, if I didn't contact you, I don't need your services." Sometimes, depending on the communication or my mood, I might mention, "If I contact you, then I look forward to seeing how your services might align with our needs and our focus." Regardless, spend as little time as possible on distractions!

It's our job as leaders to keep the focus on proven methods rather than on popular fads that undermine our goals.

Milestone 15 - Reflection and Action: Eliminate Distractions

1. How does the drone symbolize eliminating distractions?

2. Where do you find the most distractions that impact you and your employees? Explain.

3. How do you eliminate distractions? Do you have strategies? If yes, explain. If no, think of a strategy that you might use next week to eliminate distraction for you or those you lead. Explain.

4. Who do you rely on within your organization to remain focused on what is proven, not popular? How do you prevent your organization from jumping on the latest fad?

Milestone 16 - High Expectations

Leaders must have high expectations for themselves and expect everyone they lead to have high expectations, as well. High expectations must be modeled and reinforced. I know from experience that no boss, direct supervisor, or board was going to have higher expectations for me than what I placed on myself. Leaders should adamantly resist mediocrity. Good is the evil of greatness and simply being good enough is dangerous for any organization. Nothing great was ever established on a foundation of mediocrity. Always demand more from yourself than anyone else could ever expect. Lowering standards leads to negative change and decreases motivation.

Leaders should not only convey a crystal clear message of high expectations, but they should also live their expectations, constantly modeling to others in the organization the high performance they desire in each team member. Maintaining high expectations is something a leader should never apologize for. Those who rise to the challenge of high expectations are the people you want to invest in and support. Those who have a high will to improve continuously find ways to learn and grow. Conversely, those who resist clear expectations of excellence and avoid growth opportunities must be dealt with swiftly with empathy, clarity, and coaching. Find a way to dismiss, separate, and prompt them to go with the least burden on resources, both emotionally and financially.

When you think of great leaders, you think of men and women who aspired to greatness and who had high standards and expectations for themselves and for others. I believe that when you make the commitment and have the desire to behave and act consistently with the highest expectations that you know, you begin to enhance your personal power. When this motion is put into place, you become the kind of leader others admire, respect, and want to emulate. When the momentum builds, high expectations are raised, you begin to attract into your life the help, support, and encouragement of the kind of people you admire. You activate the law of attraction in the very best way. I believe the law of attraction brought one of my former athletes and me together, without a doubt!

Once in a while, if fortunate, you will lead someone that will never go...they will always be a part of your life. The law of attraction keeps you attracted. As a leader, sometimes we have a great opportunity to not only help others grow but to also learn and grow from those we lead. If you're lucky enough, you may have someone you once led that changes your life while you perhaps changed their life as well. Because of high expectations, I was blessed to see the transformation of a student-athlete I once coached. When I met Charlie he was a junior in high school. Charlie lacked self-esteem, confidence, and at times, held his head low. Charlie did not have high expectations. Charlie was a scrawny kid and didn't care much about his grades when we first met. Charlie was a victim of parents who did not provide many opportunities or much support, certainly never instilling high expectations. Surviving day to day, he certainly had not thought much about his future.

I quickly grew to love Charlie. Because of Charlie, I am a better leader and certainly a better person, father, and husband. Charlie taught me more about endurance and high expectations than I could have ever taught him. One of my favorite keynote speeches I have delivered is titled, "Who's Your Charlie?"

So, "Who is my Charlie?" Charlie was an underdog who became a champion. Charlie joined my cross country team in 1995 with no expectations. Charlie described how he had faced years of abuse and neglect by his parents, had a deadbeat father, lived in poverty, had poor self-esteem, severe acne, poor eating habits, and side effects of growing up with second-hand smoke. Charlie claimed his parents NEVER attended a school event, despite my attempts to convince or even make arrangements for them. Not only did Charlie express severe neglect and appalling lack of expectations and support within this home, but he also disclosed a history of sexual abuse. Charlie had endured much more pain and challenges than most, which made for a kid who would not easily surrender in a race when his lungs were burning, gut aching, and legs feeling heavy. Before getting Charlie to excel at running, I had to get his mindset around high expectations and working hard. I spent most of my time talking to Charlie about hygiene, making school a priority, using running to further his education in college, and developing character. I spent more time coaching and leading Charlie with lessons of life than I did coaching him through mile repeats and running hills to build his running endurance. Charlie simply needed high expectations and someone to hold him accountable with tough love. Charlie soon began to "fly" and quickly became the "gutsiest" athlete I ever coached. Charlie broke school records, won championship races, helped our team win championship events, and he became an all-state runner. The best accomplishment, due to an expectation we agreed upon together, was when he was able to be the first one in his family to attend college. Even better news....he did so on a cross country scholarship. Charlie became a student-athlete in college, something others never thought possible, including his own high school guidance counselor. Expectations are everything.

Through developing a relationship with Charlie and holding him to unrelenting high expectations, he absolutely flourished. His full potential tapped and unleashed, I thought Charlie would "run through a brick wall" for me because he knew I loved him. Without question, I cared enough about him that I would "coach through a brick wall" to help him improve as a student, young man, and as an athlete.

Charlie would endure pain, go to the well, and dig deep into the hurt zone to run as fast as he could, often out-running his competition and the challenges Charlie had endured at home. After his days of being a collegiate runner, Charlie enlisted in the U.S. Army as a way to not only continue his drive to develop character and meet high expectations, but to serve his country and to explore career opportunities while furthering his education. Sergeant Charlie served 15 years in the U.S. Army and trained in the parachute infantry for the 82nd airborne division. He battled terrorists face-to-face, serving three tours: one in Kuwait and two in Iraq.

While Charlie has since retired from the U.S. Army, he continues to struggle with his own battles, fighting the (PTSD) post-traumatic stress disorder, depression, and attempts of suicide. Charlie is married to a wonderful wife and has three children. To this day, I get to be part of Charlie's life and I am incredibly proud of the home he is providing for his own children. His three kids not only have two great parents who are instilling high expectations, but they also have a dad who knows how to endure. They have a father who endured challenges they will never face!

Milestone 16 - Reflection and Action: High Expectations

1. How does the army symbolize high expectations?

2. Who's your Charlie? Who's your underdog? Who's your student, employee, teammate, or colleague that does not fit the "norm?" Who might you lead to greatness, despite the odds being stacked against them? Who might you lead in a way that changes their life? Share your thoughts.

3. Do you live and model the expectations you desire to see in those you lead? Explain.

4. What is the perception of those you lead in regards to your expectations for them and their work? How do you know? How might you assess?

· Are your expectations high enough? How do you know?

Milestone 17 - Mistakes

Ever run naked along the coastline of an ocean? Great idea-nope!
Mistake-yes! Traveling to Gulf Shores, Alabama, our college track team
competed in a meet on the way down, trained for a week in warm sunny
conditions—free from our Michigan snow, and competed in a track
meet on the way back home. What I didn't realize was the jeopardy I put
myself into by joining some teammates on a nude beach run, carrying
our boxers in case we "ran" into bystanders.

We thought this would be a fun, rebellious adventure, but our momen-
tary thrill came to a jarring halt. Following our little jaunt, runners on
the girls' team squealed in the revelry while waving a camera in our
faces! Had they captured our incriminating escapade? We dismissed
their laughter and giggling as a joke, but the gravity of our mistake
became realized when we were called into the two assistant coaches'

condo for an impromptu meeting the next morning. Shuffling in with the weight of our shame and guilt, we knew we had made a mistake. All I could think of was my coaches calling my parents and describing the mortifying thing I had done. My stomach constricted with the fear of answering to my dad. I also panicked that I would be kicked off the team or sent home to Michigan.

Sitting in my coaches' condo, my face was aflame but my blood had turned to ice. I could hardly breathe, and looking around at my team-mates' stricken faces, it was clear we shared a common horror. My heart ached when both coaches told us how deeply disappointed and ashamed they were. They also told us, if word got out to our head coach, we would be on the first bus home to Michigan at our own expense...GULP! Our assistant coaches provided a powerful learning opportunity and later in the day, sitting on the beach, we were individually talked to by each coach to process our learning. I will never forget my coach, three-time Olympian, Brian Diemer, looking me in the eyes and saying, " Helmer, I expect more from you as a leader on this team. I will count on you to step up and lead in a positive way, moving forward." Moving forward, I refused to let my coach down after hearing of his esteemed trust in me! Lesson learned.

Sometimes we are ignorant of the brash mistakes we make until they are brought to our attention. Thankfully, I once had a Director of Business provide me with "hit me on the forehead with a two-by-four" type of feedback, I was oblivious to the mistake of sending emails after "work hours," at all times of the morning and night, and on weekends. It was not uncommon for me to fire off an email at 4:45 a.m. before a morning run and then another email after a run because I just thought of something—sometimes all to the same person, firing off emails left and right before 7:00 a.m. One time I sent a group text on an early Saturday morning, and a wonderful colleague of mine, replied back to all..."Helmer must have just finished his morning run." I am a hard worker and will work long hours, sometimes 12 - 15 hours a day, but what I didn't realize was the message I was sending to those I led. My Saturday night emails or Saturday morning text messages had unintended consequences. I was making people feel that if they were not working on weekends, before dawn, or late in the evening, they were not meeting my expectations. The two-by-four hit hard, so I immediately addressed the issue. I became much more conscientious of protecting others' personal time, respecting their email inboxes by pausing or delaying email messages unless something was urgent.

Enduring mistakes can be one of the most powerful learning lessons and growth opportunities leaders can use to their advantage. Mistakes do become failures when we continually respond to them incorrectly, but rectifying mistakes swiftly and with sincerity is an awesome way to process personal growth and model integrity to those we serve. Leaders are not perfect, but we can be humbled by our mistakes, learning and leading with a growth mindset.

High performers and organizations that promote innovation and cutting-edge thinking rely on mistakes to help guide them to success. Mistakes lead us one step closer to an intended goal through analysis and adjustment. Often, mistakes are part of the process and should be looked at as a positive. I remember my dad saying, "If you're making mistakes, then at least you're out trying to do something. Just don't make mistakes on purpose and you will be able to look at yourself in the mirror." For some reason, I have found myself looking in the mirror countless times thinking about the mistakes I have made, but feeling good about the process and how the mistakes have led me closer to my intended goal. Organizations that have leaders who use mistakes as guides to improve performance and coaching opportunities will enhance trust, innovation, and creativity. Give people expectations, parameters, and resources, then stay out their way, allowing them to make mistakes; they will flourish because of the trust that is established. My best advice on making mistakes is to recognize the mistake, admit the error, processing and learn from the experience, and then forget about it!

Milestone 17 - Reflection and Action: Mistakes

1. How does the runner symbolize making mistakes?

2. Share a recent mistake you made that led to learning and growth for you. Explain.

3. How do you react to the mistakes of others you lead? How might you provide coaching and learning lessons from mistakes?

4. As leaders, it is important to model how we acknowledge and learn from our mistakes. What is a mistake you might own and process with those you serve?

Milestone 18 - Improvement Cycles

Continuous improvement and growth are why we have leadership in organizations. Leaders of any kind should promote growth. The first step is realizing that greatness lies in the gaps between the current status and where you want to be. Developing a specific plan is the next step, which can be done with a simple guide such as "plan, do, assess, and adjust." Improvement cycles do not need to be significant, but incremental development at a steady rate is something in which leaders should develop for themselves and those they lead. Assessing progress is best captured by showing artifacts and evidence, which are critical accountability measures for leaders, teams, groups, companies, and organizations.

Improvement cycles are best established by working through the following cycle:

Plan - Do - Assess - Adjust

I will use email communication as an example of employing the (PDAA) plan, do, assess, and adjust the improvement cycle. PDAA can be used for any current status in which you would like to make improvements. As a parent, I have used PDAA to help my three boys improve the current condition of their bedroom cleanliness!

Problem: Email communication is not being utilized efficiently and effectively within our organization due to the quantity and time of email communications.

Plan

- Present factual information on how email communication can be a distraction.
- Share time allocations and the number of emails for typical people within your organization.
- Block advertisements and all marketing emails.
- Discuss when Bcc and Cc are appropriate.

Do

- Establish times of day in which you will commit to addressing email communication.
- Reduce the number of emails by calling or seeing people face-to-face.
- Do you really need to Cc someone else? Do they really need to know or even care?
- Define the improvements you would like to establish. For example,

I want to reduce sending Cc and Bcc emails by 25%.

Assess

- Count and calculate your email communications, what is the average per day/week, and record the data: pre and post PDAA.
- Ask someone who is a regular recipient of your email communication to provide feedback.

Adjust

- Make adjustments each day and each week based on your checks and feedback.
- Continue to plan, do, check, and adjust until you make the improvements desired.

Milestone 18 - Reflection and Action: Improvement Cycles

1. How does the circle symbolize improvement cycles?

2. Define an area that you would like to make an improvement in. Why?

3. Create a draft plan of a "plan, do, assess, and adjust".

4. How might you work with someone in your organization on an improvement cycle? What will your plan look like and how will you present it?

Milestone 19 - Identify Key Stakeholders

Identifying key stakeholders is incredibly beneficial for a leader transitioning into a new position. As a leader grows in the position, it is just as important to maintain positive relationships with those vital stakeholders, while also identifying new key stakeholders as the organization shifts and grows. Change in employees, team members, and key players is inevitable.

Why identify key stakeholders? To successfully lead a group of people and endure the stress and pressure of transformation, improvement cycles, and implementing systems, a leader must know the history, learn who has political power, know who has the respect and relational leverage to impact cohort groups/individuals, and who will be roadblocks. It is also important to identify the low performers and high performers and to understand how each individual enhances or undermines the team commitments.

In previous leadership positions, I have not only identified the key stakeholders but have also recorded anecdotal notes with reasons for their identification. Key stakeholders are important for seeking feedback, assessing what needs to be improved, removed, or overhauled. Once trust is established, key stakeholders will help guide leaders through critical decision-making while helping to bring others along within the organization. Leadership cannot be done by dictating or demanding, it must be carefully rolled out in a way that people feel influenced and become part of the process. When done strategically, any outcome can be accomplished with key stakeholders catalyzing the process.

When identifying stakeholders, be sure to also identify the key critics as well. While there will always be resistors, the critical mass of momentum will follow your key stakeholders. Focus on your team leaders; they will be integral in helping you drive change and impact the culture positively. Take care of these key stakeholders and protect them from resistors by constant loops of feedback, encouragement, and positive strokes of public recognition within the organization.

Leaders who demand change without a process of engaging key stakeholders will have well-intentioned plans backfire, or the organization will limp along haphazardly with the change taking no real effect, or the entire pursuit will be a guise - people faking the actions of what the leader wants to achieve. The consequence of not involving key stakeholders in the process is a failure of gaining perspective and truly understanding the fears that will need to be acknowledged and overcome by the drive strength of stakeholders. Employees faking the actions of what a leader wants is something that too many leaders are afraid to acknowledge. Because I said so, or I told the department heads to act, or I asked my 100 employees all to do it does not work. You might have compliance, but you're kidding yourself if you believe your change is truly maximizing your intended outcomes.

Enduring leadership requires constant interaction with key stakeholders. Listening to the voices of our identified key players will allow you to listen to the voice within as you guide and lead a productive process. Finally, to endure the demands of a leadership position, I recognize and encourage the need for leaders to make decisions without stakeholder input or a process. We've all made decisions that we regret later. It is generally best to get input from key stakeholders; however, sometimes a decision needs to be made about something trivial or urgent.

Whether you have a Christian faith or not, people around the world have recognized that Jesus has changed the course of human history by His leadership and development of stakeholders. His teaching and ministry began with a small group of stakeholders. Although His disciples were ordinary men, they became key stakeholders and provided Jesus with great intel of the people. The disciples joined Jesus and His message and created a movement that rapidly spread and is still spreading across the world today. Jesus spent most of his earthly ministry leading a small group. Jesus reached the masses of humanity by focusing on the few. After Jesus identified His 12 disciples, they spent time simply observing and watching Jesus lead. Jesus modeled, taught, and later, He asked His disciples to join him. His leadership, coaching, and presence became the essence of their growth and development. The key stakeholders of Jesus saw His love, care, and positive interactions with people He met and served. They witnessed how He taught in parables, how He healed, how He forgave, and most importantly, how He sacrificed. They observed Jesus gain strong followership and they became His hands and His feet in the world. People recognized the leadership of Jesus and were drawn to be influenced by His relationship.

Identifying key stakeholders will help you lead with endurance. As leaders, we need others to help us move forward. Key stakeholders can help be messengers, transformers, influencers, and communicators. Key stakeholders, like the disciples, will help leaders get to the masses!

Milestone 19 - Reflection & Action: Identify Key Stakeholders

1. How does the key symbolize identifying key stakeholders?

2. Who are your key stakeholders? Why? Create a list and explain why.

Criteria considerations: Relational leverage, professional expertise, experience, team respect, etc.

3. Identify an initiative that you could not have accomplished without the help of key stakeholders. Why was their influence so vital?

4. Will your key stakeholders change depending on the outcomes and change you're currently seeking in your organization?

5. When does a leader use positional authority to make a decision without a process or input from key stakeholders? What are some examples when you needed to make a decision as the leader in charge without input? Was it the right decision? Why?

Milestone 20 - Ask "Why" More Often

Why not ask "why?" Leaders should focus on "why" people do what they do versus "what" they do. When leaders ask the question "why" it forces those we lead to think. When asking why, and sometimes asking why several times, people reduce excuses to find the root cause of a problem. Asking "what" and "how" questions lack the narrowing focus that "why" questions do. For example, asking my boys "why" they didn't clean their bedroom allows for further narrowing. If they say, "I did clean my bedroom" I can almost guarantee I will find an area of their room that was not clean, with the exception of Hayden, our oldest son. His bedroom might be the cleanest room in our house. For our other two boys, if I look around, I can ask, "Why didn't you dust the bookshelf?" or "Why didn't you make your bed?". Eventually, the root cause for not having a well-cleaned bedroom is because they rushed due to something much more fun that they wanted to do. It has never failed me with our two youngest boys...try it!

At times, leaders may reserve caution of asking "why" because it can be considered intrusive, confrontational, and may even appear to be accusatory. Truthfully, I have made many mistakes when asking "why" because of the directness that was perceived. However, I have learned that tone of voice, gestures, facial expression, and the manner in which I frame the question negates the uncomfortableness. Many times, our intuition will inform us of the "why".

Despite leaders often being in an authoritative position, asking "why" can be utilized as a great tool for teaching, learning, growing, and thinking. Asking "why" promotes critical thinking, which may spark solutions, energy, and discovery. Depending on the topic, leaders must use their intuition to know how much time is needed for a response. Sometimes wait time, and allowing an employee to pause, think, and respond after a few minutes is appropriate. Sometimes; however, time for research, further dialogue, or brainstorming is required, and the leader needs to be respectful and in tune to knowing whether or not to press for answers.

Great leaders, just like great parents, hold people accountable. Whether it's holding your kids accountable for clean bedrooms, or a direct report for being on time to meetings, asking "why" and pressing with additional "whys" will not only ensure accountability but also solutions. Through love and logic, we can coach others to solve their own problems and access their full potential to the organization. Our love must be conveyed and perceived. Our ardent concern coupled with critical questioning can reveal the reason for not meeting an expectation, and it ultimately places the responsibility back to the individual.

High performing leaders are teachers. Leaders must realize that by asking "why" we allow those we lead to think and understand. The teaching process is a challenging one if it's going to be effective. But for great leaders, every conversation and problem provides an opportunity to create a lesson plan that will develop and grow those we serve, even if it's monitoring the cleanliness of a bedroom.

We don't live in a vacuum, and effective leaders don't allow people to languish in isolation. We are all influenced by people around us, absorbing their knowledge, gaining a broader perspective, and helping each other move forward. Asking "why" more often helps us to understand one another better. Asking "why" more often is underestimated as a leadership strategy. Asking "why" provides a quick assessment of the current status and allows a leader to seek a thorough view of how the organization is functioning and operating. Asking "why" will naturally provide opportunities for those we lead to reflect and process as well.

Sometimes, you will need to ask "why" several times, to help narrow the understanding or truly identify the root cause of the current status. While it might appear to be mundane, try asking "why" several times. When someone responds with an answer to your why questions, come back with another "why" until you have exhausted thinking and conversation. To prevent awkwardness, let the person know what you will be doing, otherwise, they will be asking why you are badgering them relentlessly. We have all witnessed an endless list of "why" questions from a 5-year-old. The curiosity of a questioning child leads to understanding, learning, and new knowledge.

While some might see a leader asking "why" as a question of one's work, as leaders, we must establish a norm for asking why as an assessment and strategy for understanding, growth, connection to employees, and seeking opportunities to improve by engaging in conversation. Asking a "why" question does not mean there is disapproval or dissatisfaction, which is the reason a leader must share the rationale of using such a strategy. We do not want employees to feel intimidated or threatened. Asking "why" more often will make it customary and comfortable.

I remember addressing a struggling department as a middle school principal simply by asking "why" during an intentional conversation, a difficult, but necessary conversation. I respected and admired our social studies department chair, a teacher who was truly a master of curriculum, lesson planning, and unit development. While I loved her passion, dedication, and continuous drive to grow and learn to better serve her students, I recognized she was floundering in her leadership with our social studies department and colleagues. It was not because she lacked the skill, it was because her plate was too full with personal obstacles that she was already enduring without the distraction of demands and attention it takes to be a department chair. While I recognized that taking care of her aging parents and terminally ill husband needed to be her focus, surrendering her role as a teacher-leader would never have happened without me asking "why" during our conversation. By asking "why" she was feeling stressed, overwhelmed, disorganized, and struggling with her role as department chair, clarity was articulated and she quickly realized how not having the demands of department chair responsibilities on her plate, she would be able to attend to her family needs and continue being the highly effective teacher she was in the classroom. Months later, she not only thanked me but wrapped her arms around me at her husband's funeral and whispered, "Thanks for being a great support to me and being real with me when I couldn't see clearly." Sometimes as leaders, we need to ask "why" to allow others to see more clearly.

Questioning and disagreeing do not mean you dislike or have ill feelings toward someone. Most questions should be asked out of care, a desire to learn, and based on a sincere intent to understand. Questioning "why," when done skillfully, can be utilized as a wonderful strategy to help and improve thinking, decision making, and leadership.

Milestone 20 - Reflection and Action: Ask "Why" More Often

1. How does the worm image symbolize asking "why" more often?

2. How might asking "why" benefit your leadership? How might you become intentional with using this particular strategy in a non-threatening way?

3. Will you need to prep your organization on the purpose of asking 'why' more often? How might you teach those you lead to ask "why" more often as a purposeful strategy?

4. Sometimes you might have to ask "why" several times to narrow down the root cause. Can you think of an example of how asking "why" 4 - 5 times can help identify the real problem? Explain.

Milestone 21 - Recruit and Retain High Performers

Hiring is one of the most important things we do as leaders! Finding the right people to hire and promote or moving existing employees into the right positions at the right time is key to human resources. Once you find your all-stars, retaining high performers becomes dependent on three things that I have found proven over and over again - culture, motivation, and impact. In the world of public education, where salaries and compensation packages do not attract candidates, I have seen how culture, motivation, and impact have not only attracted the best and brightest candidates but effectively promoted employee retention. I know of employees who took 10% - 25% compensation reductions to work in school districts that had positive cultures with synergy among administration and teachers, high levels of motivation due to learning, growth, and collaborative opportunities, and experiences of being valued and feeling they are making a difference. People desire to have a high impact on the work they do, and it's up to leaders to cultivate that type of working environment. It was embarrassing for me at times, to offer people a contract when I knew the monetary sacrifices and financial "hits" they were taking to join our organization. People are not always driven by the dollar alone!

To lead with endurance, we need high performing people by our side. Leadership is about influencing people: nothing more, nothing less! If as leaders, we are all about leading people, why would we not want the highest performers within our control to lead? Human resources and the human factor is what ultimately drives the culture of any organization. Culture will not only drive the achievement and success of any organization, but it's the people who drive your culture by how they behave, act, talk, and conduct themselves while at work and away. The responsibility of any culture lies with the leader in charge. The leader bears the burden of culture, which begins with hiring and retaining high performers.

Successful teams, businesses, and organizations are dependent upon the talent and dedication of their members, including loyalty to the organization and the leader. The talent must run deep in order to maximize success! Otherwise, you will fall apart and blow away when the pressure is on.

Our family has hunting property, located in northern Michigan. We have a wide variety of deciduous trees on our property, each tree displaying beautiful characteristics, especially the bight fall leaf colors in autumn. The most beautiful trees are the maples with the orange, red, and yellow colors that set the cloudiest day ablaze. Birch trees, poplars, and maples have great characteristics, but it's the oak tree that stands the tallest and strongest. Every year, our pathways and roadways become blocked by fallen branches, limbs, and even fallen trees, debris that comes from the shallow and short-spread root systems of trees not as mighty as the oak. On our hunting property, we have a tree stand, located about 22 feet up in a mature white oak. This particular white oak is nearly 100 feet tall with a diameter of more than 5 feet. I have hunted from this tree since 1994. While the tree continues to outgrow our tree stands, we continue to regenerate our tree stand in this mighty oak, just at it has regenerated its leaves and acorns over the years. High above the ground, this tree has survived windstorms, ice storms, hard winters, severe frosts, and even other trees falling upon its trunk and branches. While other trees have fallen dead, rotted, or become victims of the harsh ever-changing weather of Michigan, the roots of this white oak run deep. The root system of a mature oak tree can total hundreds of miles. An oak's chief support, the taproot, grows vertically for some distance. The taproot of an oak provides an anchor, before branching out into a root system that becomes embedded into the soil. The deep and widespread roots of an oak tree are the type of employee we want to recruit and retain. We want our high performers to become rooted in our organizations. Higher performers, if fertilized and watered will spread culture, motivation, and impact. When storms come, the roots will keep the organization and leader standing tall.

While trees must withstand the power of wind storms, leaders must withstand the influx of political storms that blow into our root systems when hiring people. As leaders, what we produce is simply an outcome and measurement of how well we are "fertilizing" and nurturing our root systems, our people. It is not about data-data-data by the numbers, it's all about our people-people-people. The root of all success comes from the culture of people, which will produce the "fruit of our labor"...a labor of love for our people doing the work!

For leaders, whenever we have positions to fill and hiring to do, the politics begin. Everyone seems to know the next best candidate, which is often how we end up hiring high performers, but sometimes a recommendation of a potential candidate is not in the best interest of the organization. About two years into my superintendent position, I had a potential candidate approach me about an opening within our district. It was not my practice to be involved with hiring staff in our individual buildings, as long as our building principals followed our hiring process of three interview rounds. I did not micromanage hiring, and I trusted our principals to hire their own team because I would not be directly supervising or evaluating staff at the building level. I personally knew this particular candidate and told him that it would be best to meet with the building principal instead of me, explaining that I do not influence the hiring of staff. My job is to hire high-performing principals, so they in return, hire high-performing staff to serve our students. After a week, it was clear that this potential candidate was leveraging his political connections as he met with our Human Resource Director, and in my opinion, asked community members to contact me on his behalf.

As the process moved forward, I learned that this particular candidate had advanced through the rounds and was a finalist. However, a multi-stakeholder committee and the principal became confident that they had a different candidate who was clearly their first choice. Unfortunately, the position would be offered to someone different than our well known, popular candidate that desperately wanted to work in our district. I know it was not easy to do what was right in this case for our principal. The pressure of popularity and politics had been felt and heard, but to the principal's credit, no wavering occurred...the focus was to hire the best candidate possible for our students and staff. The right decision was made.

Following the announcement, the right decision was solidified as the known candidate showed signs of bitterness and anger. We were confident our hiring process led us to the right hire, and our confidence was only validated further by the fallout of sourness clearly felt by our runner-up.

Leadership is all about influencing people. Whenever openings occur, influencing high performers to join your organization is the first step. Identifying high performers is easy, recruiting is difficult. Even though a compensation package is important, know that the culture of your organization is the most vital reason a high performing employee will join or leave an organization. Spend time recruiting, meeting, and connecting with your networks to identify recruits and then go after them with passion. For recruits in highly political positions, confidentiality is necessary to protect the process. Do not break confidentiality and remain honest when you do have to release names publically.

When recruiting, rely on those who do the work to help recruit and make connections. Not only encourage, but develop specific plans to recruit for particular positions. Relying on other high performers to recruit other high performers is often the way the network system works.

Retaining high performers is much easier if you have a strong culture and opportunities for employees to grow and learn. Keeping high performers can be a challenge. Continue to find ways to grow your high performing employees, regardless of a new position or not. Providing growth opportunities keeps people motivated. Fostering intrinsic motivation and a positive, healthy culture within your organization is the most important factor in employee retention.

Milestone 21 - Reflection & Action: Recruit and Retain High Performers

1. How does the oak tree symbolize recruiting and retaining high performers?

2. What is your current recruiting process? Do you have specific plans and procedures?

3. Do you have high levels of employee turnover? If yes, assess your culture and growth opportunities for employees. If no, why do you believe you have strong employee retention?

4. How might you improve your recruiting efforts to attract the best and brightest? Do you contact colleges, trade schools, or training organizations to ask about their best? Where can you find future candidates and how can you establish a relationship in a way that recruits are filtered and sent your way?

5. How might you grow the root systems of employees and the team by fostering an attractive culture, increasing motivation, and impacting the greater cause?

Milestone 22 - Growth

The number 22 is my wife's favorite number, so milestone 22 will begin with a leader we both love and adore...Oprah Winfrey. Oprah has impressed me as a lifelong learner, someone eager to grow and transform. We respect people who show us they are lifelong learners. Oprah Winfrey didn't produce a show in which she claimed she knew everything. She became widely respected and captured the hearts of millions because she didn't tell us what to do; she showed us her vulnerability and let America learn right alongside her. America cheered her on as she struggled with weight issues and her abusive childhood. The Oprah Winfrey Show made learning accessible and authentic, reaching into our living rooms to broaden our horizons and influence the way we live.

Oprah once said, "I am so grateful for my years of literally living in poverty because it makes the experience of creating success and building success that much more rewarding." Oprah embraced change and her mind and heart were open to the opinions of others, striving to grow, enduring the pain and suffering of life but learning along the way. Guests on the Oprah show were always inspiring and gritty—exceptional models of honor and endurance. Their stories of endurance and successful achievement of milestones became the influential highlights that attracted millions of eager viewers each day. Growth is incremental and is intended to be gratifying; leaders must celebrate not only the growth of those they lead but their own growth as well.

Are you a lifelong learner? Are you continuously learning and improving your leadership skills? Do you provide opportunities for growth for your employees to avoid stagnant behaviors and complacency? Incremental growth with just the right amount of healthy agitation is necessary for progress. Not all people are intrinsically motivated and eager to seek opportunities for improvement. However, as a leader, not only is modeling growth vital but providing a culture of learning and continuous improvement while protecting emotional safety for those you lead is critical. Growth is not just about attending a conference, taking a course, completing your continuing education credits, or joining a workshop. Growth is a mindset! Growth is a passion for improving one milestone after another, being better tomorrow than you are today. Growth is also feeling humble about what we think we know.

In 2014 when I became the Superintendent of Mona Shores Public Schools, an organization of nearly 5,000 staff and students, I recall the hesitation and resistance of shifting from Microsoft Word documents to the use of Google Docs. Before I set the expectation for our district, I doubted the need to learn a new product because Microsoft Word provided me with everything I thought I needed. Once I learned the incredible collaborative power of sharing documents, monitoring revision history, and being able to share and edit live documents, I knew that not only did I need to learn how to become an adept user of this technology, but I would need to relate the value of Google Docs and promote excitement and appreciation of this shift to our team. We also developed a long-term vision of purchasing nearly 4,000 Chromebooks for our staff and students; learning how to effectively and efficiently use Google Docs became a primary focus. Within two years, we shifted 500 employees from a Microsoft district to a Google Docs district. Through communicating our purpose, providing time to shift, developing specific training, and ensuring just in time support as well as accountability, sweeping growth occurred within all six of our district's buildings for over 500 employees.

Leaders are trailblazers and we must first navigate and master the terrain before expecting our team to charge. As torchbearers we illuminate the way for our team, guiding and coaching them to the next milestone we've journeyed ourselves. Professional learning; whether it's sharpening communication skills, developing facilitation skills to lead more productive meetings, or trying new organizational features in digital management, should be ongoing. If learning and growing no longer become a focus area for a leader, motivation will decrease and the organization will decline into stagnation.

Leaders must be visionaries who establish long-term learning and growth outcomes for the organization. Target individuals, small groups, and the whole group with learning expectations to ensure incremental growth throughout the organization. People learn in different ways and at different rates; therefore, repeat training sessions should be offered until mastery or the critical mass has accomplished the intentional goal.

When it comes to underperforming employees, if plentiful opportunities to grow are offered and the employee does not grow, the leader must determine whether growth is not occurring due to low-will or low-skill. If both, move to find a way to get the employee to go. If it's low-will, do the same. If it's low-skill and they are not making satisfactory gains, again, find a different way to help them to grow. As a leader, spend time, energy, and resources on employees that have the will to grow, learn, and improve.

The human desire to grow is innate. Parents are so proud and reel with excitement when their child recites the alphabet song. Parents are leaders simply by providing coaching, timely support, and cheerleading to their child as incremental growth occurs with every attempt at the alphabet. Low-skill is overcome by high will of the child because their leader is focused on the growth mindset. A growth mindset is that of a student eager to learn. Great leaders are lifelong learners and instill growth mindsets within their organizations. Learning is an exuberant experience. The acquisition of new skills sets the mind and soul aflame with the insatiable desire for more. Consequently, eager learners awake with purpose, joy, and excitement each day. Be an eager learner!

As leaders, we must seek and pursue growth opportunities. The best leaders I know continue to focus on personal growth and the growth of those they lead. Some practices, that I have found most beneficial to my personal and professional life, helping me to endure the demands of life and leadership include the following:

- Network with high performers that do what you do very well.
- Hire a professional coach.
- Read books, articles, and literature focused on your craft.
- Attend conferences and workshops on topics that align with your

organizational goals.
- Take time to reflect, process, and assess your leadership.
- Conduct surveys and ask for specific feedback.
- Job shadow or spend a morning or afternoon with other leaders, including leaders with similar roles and leaders from a different business or sector.
- Use social media networks to promote discussion on timely leadership topics.
- Take courses, graduate coursework, weekend cohorts, or work on a new degree.

Milestone 22 - Reflection and Action: Growth

1. How does Oprah symbolize growth?

2. How do you grow?

- List 3 - 5 strategies you use to grow/hone your craft and develop your skills.

· Checklist: Check any growth strategies below that you consistently use:

_____Take courses

_____ Hire a coach

_____ Meet with an established mentor

_____ Mentor someone else

_____ Read: Books, articles, literature, etc.

_____ Subscribe to a professional organization membership

_____ Utilize professional social media networks

_____ Other(s)

3. What are your next growth areas? How will you become trained, coached, or engaged in a growth cycle?

4. How can you identify incremental growth steps for each employee, department, cohort group, and/or levels within your organization?

5. Who in your organization, if any, is not growing and improving at the rate you desire? If you have not done your due diligence to coach, train, or provide resources to assist, it's not fair to force the employee to go. What might be the next steps you can take this week, next week?

Milestone 23 - Mindset & Drive

I believe our mindset and drive are more important than talent, education, and physical traits because success is driven by how badly we want something and how many times we're willing to get up after failure and press forward until we succeed. The power of the mind is incredible.

Conquering Tourette's is a daily battle and because I choose to focus on the variable that I can control - attitude and effort; I refuse to let a syndrome interfere with my daily life. Attitude is directly related to mindset, and effort is all about "drive". We can choose our attitudes and control our level of effort, and this is where high performing leaders separate themselves from mediocrity. I refuse to succumb to mediocrity in any aspect of my professional life, and regardless of position, those who have worked for me profess my mindset and drive to be my palpable strength and legacy.

Bearing a positive mindset energizes and invigorates others. The best leaders I know aren't simply talented, they are deeply passionate and relentless in their pursuit of positive change. Witnessing this fiery drive for the best, others simply catch the fever - the zest and glorious exertion is just too compelling! Why sit on the sidelines and surrender to the status quo when you can be part of a dynamic transformation? Leaders bring clarity of possibilities when obstacles seem insurmountable, they inspire and encourage when hearts grow weary, and they doggedly drive towards the target goal when others want to fold and quit.

Leadership has less to do with a title, rank, or *position* than it does with *disposition*. The mindset and drive of leaders is a major determinant of the culture! Inspired leaders realize that a positive mindset will drive a positive culture, which promotes high performance from the team members. Other attributes may have propelled our rise to leadership, but it is a positive mindset and drive that gives us the requisite stamina and fervor to achieve rigorous goals.

I remember learning the power of mindset and drive when being mentored by an athletic performance psychologist when I was training for the 1996 USA Olympic Trials. A small group of runners met for a mindset training session, finding a piece of string and a small gold ring on our tables. We were told that our mental strength was powerful enough to put the ring into motion just how our minds control our legs when we're pushing through the pain in the final stages of a race. Doubtful, I picked up the string and summoned my concentration. We placed the gold ring onto the string and let the ring slip to the middle, holding both ends of the string between our index finger and thumb. We couldn't believe our eyes...we were mentally moving the ring. Our psychologist and coaches used this simple exercise to demonstrate how we can run just a bit faster when tired, dig a bit deeper when hurting, and focus on moving forward with drive and energy while welcoming the pain. The power of the mind, when properly exercised, will begin to move the ring back and forth...it's simply incredible. As in life and leadership, our minds will move us forward through suffering, problem-solving, and chasing our dreams across the finish line.

A positive mindset and constant focus on driving forward will help any leader endure. Drive strength can be launched when we have an identifiable mission and vision. Similar to athletes, leaders need to have well-conditioned minds, and our minds have the ability to move a ring with nothing but thought.

Ring Activity - I encourage you to try this activity to see the power of the mind for yourself.

Materials: 10 - 12 inches of string (Sewing string is best). A ring (washers will also work).

Step 1: Place the ring on the string, and slide it down about half-way.
   Step 2: Place your elbow on a table to eliminate movement.
   Step 3: Hold the string (both ends) between your pointer finger and thumb, the ring should be less than an inch from the table, which allows you to focus better.
   Step 4: Use your other hand to steady the ring. Once it is steady, release it so that the ring is just dangling without any movement.

Now for the power of the mind!

Step 5: Focus on the ring and visualize it swinging away from and towards you. See it moving. After a minute or two, then you will notice that the ring starts moving. Remember to keep your hand still.

Of course, one might be thinking, "Hmm...it must be the airflow, a breeze, or my breathing that is causing the movement." How about we challenge such pessimistic thinking by trying the following:

Step 6: Now visualize the ring moving from side to side instead. A minute or two later you should have the ring swinging the opposite direction.

If you are still not convinced, try the following two advanced steps to demonstrate the power of the mind. Only attempt if the participant has mastered steps 5 and 6.

Step 7: Choose which direction and repeat step 4 or step 5 until you have the ring moving back and forth. Once it's moving, use complete focus to visualize the ring stopping, becoming motionless. Use your mind to push against the motion...slow that ring to a stop!

Step 8: Again, once the ring is held steady, release it so the ring is dangling without any movement. Now, with all of your focus, visualize, and see the ring moving circularly in motion.

While this particular activity is relatively simple and may seem childish, I encourage you to physically and mentally try it. Our minds are powerful. When we tell our mind to do something, we can overcome any obstacle. Despite using a table to stabilize movement, trying to keep your hand steady, your mind is focused on moving the ring. Because of your mindset and focus, your mind will move the ring by igniting tiny imperceptible vibrations in your fingers, hand, and wrist. When you focus and let your mind do its job, it will often accomplish what it chooses, what it visualizes!

When leading people, it's our charge to change the mindset of thinking...visualizing the problems we want to solve and the solutions or goals we want to create. With a deliberate focus and eliminating distractions, we have the ability to accomplish and endure more than we ever imagined. The power of narrowing the focus of our minds can move much more than a ring. Our mindsets, when focused on a clear mission, an inspiring vision, and driven by noble core values, will, in fact, move an entire organization or team.

Why do we need a mission, vision, and core values? Together, they focus on a mindset with a relentless drive to endure! Without all three, a leader does not have clarity and will make decisions that are wishy-washy. An organization without all three will flounder and never maximize its potential. A mission, vision, and core values provide drive strength and focus.

Leaders should not only think of their own individual mission, vision, and core values, but each should be recorded, communicated, written, and most importantly, lived by example. Just as important, a leader must ensure their organization has clearly developed a mission, vision, and core values.

Once identified, it's the leader's responsibility to build repetition, accountability checks, and filter all decision-making through a vetted process that includes the mission, vision, and core values. Statements are worthless unless they become embedded into individual and organizational practices on a regular, consistent basis. During my superintendency, nearly every leadership team meeting included an activity that revisited our mission, vision, or core values, simply to keep the team mindset focused and our drive aligned. If your key stakeholders do not know and make decisions based on your mission, vision, and core values, leadership has failed.

A mission statement should be brief, memorable, and a catchphrase that defines what you and your organization will do. A vision statement should be a challenge, a movement statement focused on what you and the organization seek or inspire to become. Both the mission and vision should be brief enough to make it easy to memorize, restate, and reference. Finally, core values, which should be no more than three to five, are great reminders of what character traits are ... non-negotiable.

When I was Superintendent at Mona Shores Public Schools, through the process of developing a four-year district strategic plan, our Board of Education adopted the following statements and core values to help focus the organization's mindset and drive.

Mission Statement: Inspiring excellence, building character, and impacting the future through academics, arts, and athletics.

Vision Statement: Mona Shores Public Schools will continue to be the premier PreK-12 educational destination in the county, state, and nation.

Core Values: Integrity, respect, perseverance, and collaboration.

Milestone 23 – Reflection and Action: Mindset & Drive

1. How does the target symbolize mindset and drive?

2. How does the ring activity demonstrate the power of the mind? How might you use this activity to connect with a particular outcome or message you're attempting to accomplish with your team or organization?

· When will you demonstrate it?

· What will be your message?

3. Define your personal mission, vision, and list of core values.

4. What are your organization's mission, vision, and core values? If non-existent at this time, how will you engage stakeholders to develop? When?

5. How might you provide repetition and keep the mission, value, and core values alive? When might it be time to revise?

Milestone 24 - Artifacts and Evidence

True or false: What doesn't get measured doesn't get done? True! Accountability drives motivation and leaders must develop a variety of modes to hold people accountable. Accountability has nothing to do with micromanaging, but rather providing a driver to keep the people we lead equipped with clear expectations of how their work will be measured. Weak leadership will allow others to simply talk about their progress without showing artifacts and evidence. While artifacts and evidence can be demonstrated with a lot of freedom, autonomy, and even creativity, agreed-upon measures should be clearly identified by the leader and those being led.

Presenting artifacts and evidence provides relevance and authenticity to the results produced. As a leader, engaging employees with identifying specific artifacts and evidence is a powerful strategy, and conducting scheduled reviews for the employee to show artifacts and evidence should be scheduled based on the uniqueness of the work being produced. Depending on the work, it could vary from hourly to bi-annually.

Fence line checks are what I refer to as a quick accountability check to be sure your guidelines are being established with fidelity. To keep the cattle safely contained, farmers regularly check the fence lines to ensure there are no fallen trees, broken posts, or damaged wires. The electricity needs to be on to keep the cattle from going astray. As with leadership, we must conduct frequent fence line checks to ensure those we lead are working within the organization's parameters; however, within the fence line, there is a lot of freedom and autonomy. Based on my experience, the practice of producing, selecting, and sharing the evidence is mutually beneficial for the employee and the leader; this practice helps leaders recognize the employee's specific contributions, provides accountability for progress, allows deeper understanding and appreciation for how team members grow the organization, helps employees focus on their personal and team goals, and showcases how specific training or professional development has been utilized. Over the years, I recall meeting with teachers to review artifacts and evidence or "celebration folders" as we called them. During mid-year reviews, I was often beaming with pride seeing firsthand great product examples that I would've never known simply by conducting classroom observations. Teachers were eager to share their work in an authentic, meaningful way that brought value to the evaluation process. Folders contained information such as email communication to parents, copies of weekly newsletters, notes from colleagues, parents, and students, a newly designed unit, terrific examples of student work, and assessment results.

Without artifacts and evidence, it is difficult for a leader to determine exactly how successful the employee is in meeting the defined target goals; this healthy agitation is the pressure that produces progress. Similarly, if a farmer kills the power to the fence, the cattle will push, nudge, and roam beyond their defined boundaries. Whatever you want as a leader, be sure to be clear on your expectations, assess and monitor work frequently until it's mastered, provide clear feedback, and be sure to have clarity on artifacts and evidence—how the expectations will be measured!

Consider the following example as a fenceline check failure. To clarify, this is a real story right from my own home as an example of what happens when the fence line is not monitored, a leadership failure with my three boys. Our sons have their bedrooms upstairs and they share a bathroom. Okay, you probably already know where I am going with this example...boys and a bathroom, right? From the time our boys were little, my wife and I made it an expectation not to urinate on the toilet rim. It sounds like a reasonable expectation, right? I cannot begin to count the broken record syndrome we have used with this expectation. We have failed time after time despite the artifacts and evidence. They would desperately deny the inaccuracy with "I didn't do it!" but the disgusting evidence spoke of their performance: urine on the toilet seat, urine splashed on the floor, the smell of urine, and urine even stained under the seat. If you have a home of daughters, be thankful you don't have this problem. Had my wife and I made the expectations clear? Yes, we had repeated the expectation over and over again. While our expectation had been clear: Keep the toilet seat clean, we had not checked the fence line. Our "cattle", the three boys in this example, continued to not only press against the fence line, but they also ventured outside the fence line after a new round of toilet cleaning occurred. Sure, the toilet seat might remain clean for a use or two, perhaps even for 24 hours, but eventually, the urine returned to the seat. Why? While I am not taking the responsibility off of our kids, I do fault myself and the lack of leadership on my part. After putting up a good fight, my wife finally surrendered, turned in her pee cleaning towel, and placed the responsibility on me to train the boys.

I do expect a clean seat when they leave the toilet. I know the solution to the problem will require constant monitoring, assessing, feedback loops, and fence line checks. However, now that I have made this public and have totally embarrassed my three kids, perhaps the electricity is turned back on with another attempt to keep the "cattle," within the fence line.

Milestone 24 - Reflection and Action: Artifacts and Evidence

1. How does the tape measure symbolize artifacts and evidence?

2. How do you hold your employees accountable by requiring them to produce artifacts and evidence?

3. What artifacts and evidence does your organization show to demonstrate progress towards organizational goals?

4. Where might you strengthen the need to identify and determine specific artifacts and evidence to improve performance within your organization or with a specific person?

5. How might the practice of producing, selecting, and sharing the evidence be mutually beneficial for both the employee and the leader?

6. What are some of your fence lines that currently need frequent monitoring and feedback to ensure the "cattle" remain within the boundaries you have established as the leader?

Milestone 25 - 5 P's

5 P's - Proper Preparation Prevents Poor Performance. When I coached cross county, at times, I would have a kid tell me, "Coach, I want to be a state champ". I loved hearing those words, but it was rare that a kid would actually have the will and the desire to prepare to be a state champion. During the winter of 2000, one of my former athletes called me and asked if he could stop by for a visit as he had a question. I had coached this athlete since 6th grade but had accepted my first administrative job the year before his senior year. Shortly after the fall season of cross country, I received a phone call from Jay Brown, now Dr. Jason Brown. Jay stopped by my house as he told me he had a question. I was curious to know what question Jay was pondering...what advice I could give him. When Jay and I sat on the deck of our home, he asked, "HOW do I prepare this offseason to be the state champ in the 800 meters?". He didn't say "Coach, I want to be a state champ".

Instead, he asked HOW do I prepare? At that point, I knew all I had to do was plan out his winter training schedule and Jay would do the work. About seven months later, in June of 2001, I stood along the fence at the state championships in Forest Hills, Grand Rapids, MI, about 100 meters from the finish line with Jay's parents, and we watched HOW Jay's preparation led him to a state championship and a scholarship to Michigan State University. It wasn't what Jay did on the day of state championships, it was HOW he prepared each day, week, month, and every year since he was in sixth grade that allowed him to accomplish his dream!

As Bobby Knight, one of college basketball's most intense coaches, once stated, "We talk in coaching about 'winners' - Kids who just will not allow themselves or their team to lose. Coaches call that a will to win. I don't. I think that puts the emphasis in the wrong place. Everybody has a will to win. What's far more important is having the WILL to PREPARE to WIN".

The little things are HUGE when preparing. Visualizing the successful execution, thoughtfully reviewing every detail, obtaining and organizing needed materials, practicing the performance and then altering it—the preparation investment all occurs when no one is watching. For example, when employing the 5 P's for staff meetings, are the supplies on the table? Is the technology cued and has the presentation been rehearsed? Are there plugins available for participants? Did your secretary prepare the copies and are they in order of flow in regard to the agenda? Is the food scheduled to be on time? Are the refreshments on the table and ready for guests as they arrive? Will there be music playing when guests enter, music that is potentially connected to the theme or the outcomes stated on the agenda? Was the agenda sent at least three days in advance? Is the furniture arranged in a way that is most conducive to learning? What about lighting? Will the sun need to be shaded; will it interfere with the projector? How will you greet each colleague or participant as they enter the room? The little things are HUGE when it comes to preparation, when it comes time to perform.

My middle son, Jackson, has some ambitious goals for his own running. After a consistent summer of training prior to his 8th-grade season, despite rehabbing a nagging injury, he became the city champ, setting a course record, and earned a medal in Kenosha, Wisconsin at the Foot Locker Midwest Regional Championships. On both days, comments were made about Jackson's great race, but he and I knew that while he performed incredibly well, it was his 5 P's that made all the difference. The bystanders did not see his daily routine of running in the heat and humidity, cross-training by swimming laps, riding an elliptical machine as he nursed an injury, doing strength training sessions every other day, stretching before school, massage therapy, attending cross country camps, drinking water instead of soda, and running in the rain or before church due to family obligations. It was Jackson's will to prepare to win that made the difference when it was time to perform. And perhaps, Jackson has heard the story about Jay Brown a time or two...

The 5 P's...Proper Preparation Prevents Poor Performance. Preparation is time proactively spent on planning, organizing, and preparing for an intended outcome. As with any goal, it's all about the journey; the plan and process that leads to high performance. Proper planning prevents poor performance (the 5 P's) is a slogan I use to serve as a reminder when considering any leadership initiative, goal, meeting, or task.

When we compare ourselves against others, we may become bitter. When we compete against ourselves, we become better. I have found this with people at work and with friends. Jealousy comes from competing against people. Look in the mirror...that's your competition. The "competition" is all about the 5 P's. To compete, we must prepare and prepare well!

On numerous occasions, I have been asked about my biggest challenges as an educational leader. While I have experienced the stress of negotiating employee contracts, finding ways to balance a 37 million dollar budget, eliminating positions due to budget constraints, terminating staff, and the middle of the night calls about a boiler going down or a pipe bursting and a flood of water damaging resources, or the irate parent appealing a discipline or code of conduct matter...THERE IS NO CHALLENGE more difficult to endure than a teenage suicide. As a leader, preparing to heal a school community directly connected to the emotional trauma of overcoming teenage suicide, without a doubt, has been my biggest challenge as an educational leader.

Sadly, I have encountered far too many suicides and attempts in my career. While each situation is tragic, two particular situations come to mind, not to minimize the other losses, but these two were within one year and in the same school community. Due to the close proximity and both involving self-inflicted gunshot wounds, it was my focus of 5 P's that helped our community heal the best we could, considering the shock and raw emotions that come to the forefront of unexpected deaths. The majority of middle school-aged students have not lived long enough to deal with the loss of a loved one, certainly not the death of a classmate. Middle school-aged kids live as immortals and when a classmate's desk is empty due to an unexpected tragedy, it changes them. For some, the change is lifelong!

As a middle school principal, I had the heartbreaking experience of dealing with two suicides and I continue to think and pray for the families involved...such great people!

Both boys were in eighth grade, 13 -14 years old. Both boys departed this world way too soon and left a community in shock and in mourning for years to come. There is simply no logical explanation of why, a smart, kind-hearted, witty eighth-grader would take a shotgun on what was a typical Sunday afternoon and shoot himself while in his bedroom. There's no way to explain the unexplainable – including why another eighth-grade boy, happy, athletically gifted, and well-liked at home and at school had used a handgun to take his own life inside his bedroom just over a year before. Two boys...two great kids full of life and not showing any signs of mental health issues. Both teenage boys departed our world, leaving behind families who were dropped to their knees in shock and pain, and a school community jolted with grief by two suicides in two years.

Based on previous crisis management I had faced in previous districts, I knew that to endure such tragedies, my leadership would be dependent upon others and my mindset of the 5 P's would be my driving force! Leading an entire school community through two unexpected teenage deaths would require endurance. Both tragedies left me working around the clock, preparing and planning a wide variety of communications, ensuring support groups were in place, tapping into community re-sources, assisting our counselors with grieving rooms, meeting with pastors and clergy, and attempting to bring normalcy back to the school setting as soon as possible. I needed to remain focused and emotionally strong, to carefully calculate and implement a plan that our crisis team could enact for the hours, days, weeks, and months ahead.

Because our crisis team came together and spent time preparing detailed steps with constant assessing, we performed our duties and navigated through the grieving process as best we could, considering the pain we were all facing. Before briefing and debriefing sessions, I closed my office door to rehearse my message so I could effectively communicate and lead. Following each rehearsal, I asked a colleague to listen to my message again, seeking feedback and making adjustments so I could do the best job possible when facing the staff and students, or clicking send on a variety of communications. Proper preparation is key when dealing with raw emotions on such a large scale as losing a teenage student during the school year. Proper preparation was also needed in order to be fully aware and respectful of our beloved families dealing with the loss of a child. A leader must prepare communication that provides clarity, support, sensitivity, and specific resources, while also protecting people during a vulnerable phase. The fear is copycat behaviors.

While being strong for those I needed to lead, it was in the quietness of my office that I would break down. I remember crying uncontrollably...I needed time to grieve as well, and based on leading other crisis plans in the past, I could not do this alone. Leaders must rely on others.

The death of an innocent young teen should raise questions of mental health, and why kids would take such acts to end their lives. Were there any adverse childhood experiences (ACEs) that impacted their mental health? In each situation, our staff reached out to the families to seek answers as to whether or not they were bullied, teased, or had issues that we clearly missed at school. We had staff that knew the boys very well and they naturally had guilty feelings, fearing they had missed a sign. Both families were clear that experiences at school had nothing to do with their child's death. Again, there is no way to explain the unexplainable.

Regardless, our crisis team at school decided to put into effect a "watch list" we had been discussing on numerous occasions. Working together with a variety of stakeholders, we made our best attempt to identify students who were struggling – whether academically, behaviorally, or emotionally. Our staff became very sensitive and this helped us move forward, feeling like we were doing something within our control, carefully monitoring our students for those who may need extra support. While we initiated the "watch list," based on what we knew, both of our boys' names would have not been placed on the list. There were no red flags on the outside, but it's very difficult to see inside the mindset of a teenager.

When asked by the community, I repeated the following statement over and over again. "Middle school kids are going through some of the most difficult times in their lives because of all the things happening to them physically — hormonally with puberty — and also with the questions of "Where do I belong? Am I loved? What group of kids do I connect with?"". While we can prepare for any situation once we know, I am grateful for the tremendous job of so many caring and giving individuals who assisted us with our crisis team and my leadership during these two tragedies. Having the mindset of 5 P's is not the solution, but rather a call to action. Although our community became closer, sometimes as you move forward, the reflection in the mirror does not look the same.

I am grateful for the mindset of 5 P's... "Proper Preparation Prevents Poor Performance" while planning for a crisis rollout, allowing me to endure leadership and "performing" my job duties and responsibilities to my best ability. To this day, each of these boys are still part of my reflection, and I know based on first-hand experiences, their lives, while way too short, positively impacted many lives and will forever live in the hearts of many!

177

Milestone 25 - Reflection and Action: 5 P's - Proper Preparation Prevents Poor Performance

1. How does the medal symbolize 5 P's - proper preparation prevents poor performance?

2. How can the 5 P's serve as a reminder to you or your organization?

3. Where have you failed due to a lack of preparation? How did you rectify it?

4. How do the success stories of Jackson and Jay relate to leading with endurance?

5. Who monitors 5 P's for quality assurance within your organization? How?

6. How does having the mindset of 5 P's help during significant, unexpected events (such as leading a community through suicide trauma) to a routine, known task (such a facilitating or preparing for a meeting)?

Milestone 26 - Relationships

When leaders value relationships and focus on cultivating a healthy culture above all else, they will realize their greatest gains in performance and achievement. Too often, leaders get caught up in the wrong data. Performance is not about the "number" data; it's all about the "people" data!

Leadership is influencing others in a positive way, leading others by the synergy of relationships. Leadership is all about people; connecting, inspiring, motivating, and growing people to get results. Far too often, leaders will find themselves focusing on the outcomes and results with spending far too little on the relationships of the people being led.

When thinking of a high performing leader in your past, you might not remember the specifics of everything they did in regards to outcomes and accomplishments, but without a doubt, you remember how they made you feel and how you connected with them through the power of a positive, healthy relationship. Leaders spend time learning how to work with people and how to treat people in a way that inspires them. On the flip side, leaders must terminate or remove people who are toxic to relationships within the organization after substantial attempts to grow, coach, and improve.

Relationships greatly impact not only the culture of an organization but the performance of those within the organization. Focusing on the culture, developing relationships, spending time connecting with employees, and purposely building systems to strengthen relationships within the organization is essential. Human beings are relational. We spend the majority of our wakened hours on work: getting ready in the morning, commuting, and often eight hours or more per day at work; the bottom line is that relationships and culture will play a significant role in not only performance but also recruiting and retention of high performing employees.

My oldest son, Hayden, has taught me a lot about relationships. At age 18, Hayden continues to amaze me with how he spends his time, focusing on relationships with people that truly matter. Although Hayden has his driver's license, he prefers to spend his time with his closest friends and family, rather than going to parties, large group gatherings, or even school events such as a Friday night basketball game. Hayden has authentic, close-knit relationships with those he really loves and appreciates, and he would much rather spend an afternoon with his nana and papa or drive over to his grandma and grandpa's house to spend time with them. Rather than sitting in the sanctuary at church, Hayden prefers to spend time with the toddlers at church, volunteering in the youth ministry. He likes to develop and maintain deep relationships with few rather than knowing many. In the fall of his sophomore year of high school, I learned he joined the knitting club, the "Knit Wits" because he truly enjoyed the teacher and the small group of students that met in a classroom rather than a large, noisy cafeteria. While he laughed at first when he found out he couldn't just hang out in there, but really had to learn to knit, he quickly relied on his teacher and his nana as they gave him tips. Just like his nana used to do, Hayden is currently knitting scarves for those he loves. When he was in elementary school, Hayden would rather do projects, run errands, or assist the librarian or his teachers during recess rather than play on the playground. He finds an incredible amount of value in connecting and getting to know his teachers and the adults in his life. He buys unique, special gifts that are heartfelt because Hayden enjoys getting to know people, and I have often heard his teachers attest to the special bond they have with him.

Hayden has taught me to value our family and friends. Hayden has enjoyed special trips with his grandma, traveling to North Carolina to visit the Biltmore Estate. He has adventured up the Chicago River to observe and learn about the architectural features of Chicago, learning right along with his grandma and aunt. Last summer, they traveled to Niagara Falls, carefully planning a detailed itinerary for each day. It's Hayden's relationship with his grandma that reminds me of the relationship I had with my grandma. My Grandma Ray lived as an angel, and to this day, she remains an angel watching over me every night as I have her framed picture on my nightstand next to my bed. She taught me how to play golf, we rode bikes together, and she assisted me with my business of mowing lawns in her trailer park, beginning at the age of 12. She took care of our house when my parents were working. She was the first noise I heard in the morning, singing with her sweet little voice, "It's time to get up, it's time to get up, it's time to get up in the morning," and she was also the first person my sister and I would see when we came home from school. Walking in the door, an after school snack was always waiting on the table. I spent many weekend nights with my grandma, even into my high school years. I believe Hayden has an angel in his grandma and nana as well, relationships that will last in his heart forever!

With my leadership positions, I have had to develop relationships with large groups, join service and leadership clubs such as rotary, attend large social events, and fundraisers. I know many people, but the connections and conversations are surface and not real. I need more of Hayden's focus in my life, and for the leaders that I have worked closest with during my years as an educational leader, I know well. As a leader, if you want to lead people, you must have a relationship of trust, respect, and care!

Two people, two leaders who been real with me for years, happen to have the name of Greg as well. Greg Gould has been a friend of mine, and a training partner (running buddy) since 1987 and Greg Pratt has been a friend and a colleague since 1995.

Greg Gould, known as "Big Greg" has been like a big brother since we were on the cross country team in 1987. Big Greg was a senior, chasing after the school record, a well-respected cross country runner, an incredible student, and a very focused leader. I was a scrawny, punk sophomore, first-year runner, who didn't even know how far 5 kilometers was, the distance of our high school races. We were each other's best man when we got married, we have traveled all around the midwest running races together, and we have endured the race of life together, one milestone after another. As of 2019, our guess is that we have logged at least 10,000 miles together. Believe me, you get to know someone when spending uninterrupted time together as we have over the years, running in snow, rain, unbearable heat and humidity, in the dunes along the shoreline of Lake Michigan, and just about every road in Muskegon County. Our friendship is a bond connected through running, and we will run together as long as our bodies allow. We have covered just about every topic known to mankind during our runs together. And when the finish line does occur, I am sure we will either walk together with canes or wheel together in wheelchairs...we will continue to endure life and leadership together, causing a little physical pain that feels so good, knowing that you're enduring life and leadership together through a special relationship.

The other Greg in my life, Greg Pratt, has remained a personal and professional friend as we instantly connected when we taught together at Orchard View Middle School in the mid-1990s. The "Pratt-Man" and I have both endured some life obstacles in educational leadership for over 25 years. Despite the distance, we have supported each other in our roles as school administrators, connecting and sharing stories, brainstorming, seeking input and advice, and at times, mourning together. I also was able to help Greg and his family move from their home in Kent City to Lowell, Michigan where he has remained the superintendent for the past eleven years. Greg and his wife, Liz, along with their two boys, Garrett and Grant, know how to endure and have experienced incredible resilience due to some health issues they have faced in their family. Liz was diagnosed with breast cancer in the summer of 2012. It was followed by a double mastectomy, radiation, and chemotherapy. Her cancer is in remission. Grant was diagnosed with acute lymphoblastic leukemia, commonly known as A.L.L in November of 2015 and continues chemotherapy today. He has a good prognosis and a great attitude. Through the power of relationships and God's grace, the Pratt Family continues to shine and make a positive difference in their community. I will forever consider Greg and his family heroes and some of the most humble, hard-working, and mentally strong people I know. The entire Pratt family represents what *LwE* is all about, and they live it each day!

The impact of a leader is based on their relationship with others. Just take a moment and think of the best leaders in your life, just like the best teachers in our lives...it's ALL ABOUT relationships!

Milestone 26 - Reflection and Action: Relationships

1. How does the heart symbolize relationships?

2. How do you purposely develop relationships with those you lead?

3. What is your definition of healthy relationships between you and those you lead?

4. How are you providing consistent ways to develop relationships within your organization?

5. How might you increase the focus on relationships and culture within your sphere of control?

6. Where are some relationships faltering? How will you improve?

The Ultimate Milestone (.2) The Finish Line Push - Passion and Energy

Symbolically, it is fitting that a "." (period) comes at the end of the 26 miles of a marathon. Once a runner reaches 26 miles, they are greeted by the crowd and cheered on to finish the last two-tenths of the race. A period generally means the end of something, which also means it can be the start of something new . . . A "." can also mean a dot or point. They can both be defined as a small mark. As leaders, we must go out into the world and make small marks that help those we serve.

26.2 . . . The finish line is an exciting thing to see after hours of running in a marathon. The .2 stands for something we often forget to do in life and leadership: celebrate. As a runner crosses the finish line of a marathon, whether it took them two hours or nine hours, they feel a sense of accomplishment and have completed something that no one can take away from them. It is time to celebrate. We celebrate with high fives, with glasses of beer, with medals, and with ceremonies. As a leader, it is important to remember to celebrate the accomplishments of those you lead. Have fun, give away medals, and be sure to take the time to celebrate the suffering along the way. Take time to celebrate when the team has endured.

Over the years, I recall multiple celebrations as a leader. While often simple by nature, it's critical to take the time to recognize hard work, effort, and endurance! From bringing out a cooler of beer and bottles of wine at the conclusion of a nine-hour administrative planning retreat to bringing in a surprise venti latte from Starbucks to a secretary who goes above and beyond, celebrating is needed. From bringing in donuts and rolls from the local bakery to celebrate a "90 Day Challenge" of enduring a focus on health, fitness, and well-being to taking an hourly paid custodian out for breakfast because he takes pride in clean front entrances and bathrooms, celebrating shows appreciation. Whether it's leaving a handwritten note on an employee's desk for turning in an exemplary report to doing a toast for passing a $13,000,000 bond project with organizational stakeholders, celebrating also builds endurance. Like crossing the finish line of a marathon, celebrating honors the suffering that comes along with our journey in life and leadership.

Regardless of the races you will run in life and leadership, use the milestones of *Lead with Endurance (LwE)* to help you in the journey. Life and leadership are about the process. *LwE* is all about mindset: it's a will, a drive to succeed, a mission to finish the race, learning and growing from each milestone along the way, and when we "Lead with Endurance", the impact is life-changing, and the finish line is celebratory. Once recovered, get back into another process and into the next race. Suffer gladly!

Bibliography

Blanchard, Ken ... [and others]. *Whale Done! : the Power of Positive Relationships.* New York: Free Press, 2002.

Collins, Jim, and James C. 1958- Collins. *Good to Great and the Social Sectors: A Monograph to Accompany Good to Great: Why Some Companies Make the Leap- and Others Don't.* [Boulder, Colo.]: Jim Collins, 2005.

Gold, Todd. *Michael Jackson: The Man in the Mirror.* London: Sidgwick & Jackson, 1989. Print.

Gordon, Jon. *The Energy Bus: 10 Rules to Fuel Your Life, Work, and Team With Positive Energy.* Hoboken, N.J.: Wiley, 2007.

Haerle, Tracy. *Children with Tourette Syndrome, A Parent's Guide.* Rockville, MD: Woodbine House, Inc., 1992.

About the Author

Greg Helmer has a B.A. in Education from Calvin College (1994) in Grand Rapids, Michigan and an M.A. in Leadership from Western Michigan University (1997). In 2012, he represented the State of Michigan as the MEMSPA Outstanding Practicing Principal of the Year. In 2013, he was invited to Washington D.C. as he was named a National Distinguished Principal of the Year by the NAESP. In 2016, he was inducted into the Hall of Fame at Orchard View Public Schools. During his career of 25 years in public education, he has served in multiple leadership roles; including teacher, coach, assistant principal, elementary principal, middle school principal, assistant superintendent, and superintendent. Greg is happily married to his wife of 21 years and they are raising three sons in West Michigan.

Epilogue

After resigning as Superintendent of Mona Shores Public Schools, I was given the gift of time to focus on writing my first book, *Lead with Endurance*. At the time, I was clueless about how scarred my reputation would be when seeking positions in educational leadership due to the politics and baggage I would carry into the interview process. After being rejected 108 times with job applications, and failing to obtain a position despite 25 interviews, it was clear that it would take a miracle, and endurance unlike ever before, to redeem me in the profession of public education. I wondered if finding a job that would not disrupt my family would be possible. Moving and/or relocation was not a favorable option. While I discovered the private sector to be much more forgiving, and lucrative with compensation, I refused to give up finding my place in education. I prayed for a position that would be a perfect fit for me personally and professionally.

Taking a high-level administrative job across the state or out of state were all options. My faith, patience, and endurance were being challenged for nearly ten months of rejections. On numerous occasions, I was told I was the "first" choice or even the "perfect" fit, but the timing and the proximity of my resignation, due to the publicity, ended up being a significant roadblock. Despite no intentional wrongdoing, my reputation had been tarnished. As we know in the world of education, the peak opportunity for new positions is between April - June. On the first day of school in the fall of 2018, it was painful to watch my 3 boys head off to school and my wife head off to her job as a teacher. For the first time since I was in kindergarten, I did not have a first day of school. I felt like a failure. No job going into a new school year meant I had missed the ample hiring window and the odds were against me. Would I have to "settle"? In the three school districts I previously worked, each organization offered me opportunities for promotions based on my impact and ability. After 108 rejections, I wondered if I might not ever see another school during my professional career.

But then the miracle happened. Two weeks into the school year, I interviewed three rounds for a teaching position, including teaching a lesson with a 5th-grade group of students, at Ravenna Middle School, located just 20 minutes east of our home. Gratefully, I started teaching English Language Arts in the 5th and 8th grades during the fall of 2018. I fell in love with teaching once again. I fell in love with the students. After nearly 20 years of school administration, I found the break I needed. Little did I know how powerful my time as a teacher would be for me. While many of my former colleagues (administrators) thought I was nuts for going back to the classroom, my spirit was rejuvenated, and my perspective was awakened with how complex the world of teaching has become since I left in the classroom in 1999 to pursue educational leadership positions.

I humbly, yet gratefully accepted a teaching position for a total compensation of nearly $150,000 less than my previous position as superintendent. Despite the significant difference in compensation, I felt alive and was learning each day. I was prepared to teach for at least three years. From the lesson plan and unit development to managing students with adverse childhood experiences, I was building a dynamic classroom environment, and I was having FUN!

Little did I know, I found myself in a building that was surprised by the news of our principal announcing her resignation the morning following our holiday break. I was asked to interview for the position by many of my teaching colleagues, and I quickly found myself in front of the Ravenna Board of Education, accepting the role of Principal at Ravenna Middle School. Sadly and disheartening, a former consultant and person involved with the collusion at Mona Shores, made several attempts to derail the board from hiring me as their principal.

How much more nonsense would I have to endure?

Just as I hit my stride in my new role as principal, the Ravenna Board of Education announced that they would not be renewing our super-intendent's contract. Unimaginable. Would I consider the position? Would the board consider me as a candidate? After spending a lot of time reflecting, praying, discussing with several of my mentors, and talking with my family, I decided to formally apply. During the first round of interviews, in front of a room full of community members, I was comfortable and felt great about the experience. I was asked to return for a final round, along with another finalist. We started the 2nd round of interviews with an informal community meet and greet. I was once again shocked when one of the board members stated, "The crazy consultant you dismissed at Mona Shores contacted me again. She has some serious nerve to reach out to me on Easter Sunday to try to persuade me to not vote for you." I was minutes away from interviewing in front of another room full of community members, forced to quickly shift my thinking just hearing that once again, evilness was trying to desperately derail me from a great opportunity, a great fit.

I was not offered the job...the other finalist was offered the position. Another rejection. Another race to endure. A few days later, the other candidate accepted a different position, and the board of education wanted to know if I was still interested. I asked for some time to do more praying, thinking, and reflecting. In the end, I would have regretted not reentering the race. Rejection? Politics? In the end, the timing was perfect. The position is perfect for my skill set and I am enjoying my next adventure, one milestone at a time.

I do believe in miracles. The mindset to endure is powerful! Who could've ever predicted I would've gone from one of the largest school districts in our county as the superintendent to one of the smallest school districts in our county as a teacher? Who could've imagined that within about seven months, I would be making transitions from teacher to principal, and finally to the superintendent?

Live and lead with endurance...I am excited for my new role... a fresh perspective of teaching and the principalship. I am committed to removing the unnecessary distractions for our educators so we can focus on what is right with public education...teaching & learning, making an impact on future generations by leading with endurance for those I serve!

Professional Learning Services

Coaching, Speaking, and Consulting

- Technical leadership
- 26.2 Milestones for Improving Life and Leadership
- Enduring personal and professional struggles while improving performance
- Strengthening personal and/or professional endurance
- Harassment, bullying, and retaliation in the workplace
- Keynote speaker
- Facilitator of learning for workshops, retreats, seminars, professional learning, and team development
- Strategic planning
- Building synergistic teams

Contact Greg:
Website: www.leadwithendurance.com
Email: *helmergreg404@gmail.com*

Made in the USA
Coppell, TX
12 January 2020

14413909R00125